A-Z of Reiki

Bronwen and Frans Stiene

Authors of
The Japanese Art of Reiki,
The Reiki Sourcebook and
Reiki Techniques Card Deck

Founders of the International House of Reiki
www.reiki.net.au
info@reiki.net.au

T0159519

JOHN HUNT PUBLISHING

First published by O-Books, 2006
O-Books is an imprint of John Hunt Publishing Ltd., 3 East St.,
Alresford, Hampshire SO24 9EE, UK
office@jhpbooks.com
www.johnhuntpublishing.com
www.o-books.com

For distributor details and how to order please visit the
'Ordering' section on our website.

Text copyright: Bronwen and Frans Stiene 2006

ISBN-13: 978 1 90504 789 5
ISBN-10: 905047 89 4

A CIP catalogue record for this book is available from the British
Library.

UK: Printed and bound by CPI Group (UK) Ltd, Croydon, CR0 4YY
US: Printed and bound by Thomson-Shore, 7300 West Joy Road,
Dexter, MI 48130

We operate a distinctive and ethical publishing philosophy in all
areas of our business, from our global network of authors to
production and worldwide distribution.

A-Z of Reiki

Bronwen and Frans Stiene

Authors of
*The Japanese Art of Reiki,
The Reiki Sourcebook* and
Reiki Techniques Card Deck

Founders of the International House of Reiki
www.reiki.net.au
info@reiki.net.au

BOOKS

Winchester, UK
Washington, USA

Praise for Books by Bronwen and Frans Stiene

A-Z of Reiki

Clear, concise, informative and easy to use, *A to Z Reiki* is a valuable reference book for every Reiki practitioner's library.

Kathleen Prasad, co-author Animal Reiki

I simply treasure this simple, yet comprehensive A-Z Reiki pocketbook, and I will keep it handy.

Inamoto Hyakuten, Japanese Reiki Master and Founder Komyo Reiki Kai

The Japanese Art of Reiki

This book feels like a sacred manuscript.

Corwin Bell, creator of Journey to Wild Divine

A gem for anyone on a spiritual path and essential for all Reiki practitioners.

Akhila Hughes, publisher of A to Zen Magazine

This book is truly a gift to the international Reiki community.
Kathleen Prasad, author of Animal Reiki

The Reiki Sourcebook

I love your book, The Reiki Sourcebook!! You have done an excellent job of research and writing for this sensitive but important material. Thank you for your meticulous effort to provide unbiased information on Reiki, which will help to keep Reiki from drowning in controversy and ego.
Nina Paul, author of Reiki for Dummies

What an incredible work. There is so much I would want people to read.
Mari Hall, author of Practical Reiki, Reiki for Common Ailments, Reiki for the Soul

The Reiki Sourcebook is a gift to humanity.
Neil Anthony, UK Reiki Federation Chair 1997-2002

Preface

Thank you to everyone who has supported this book from its infancy through to its maturity, especially you – the reader.

Deepest thanks to our families and friends who continue to support us on our own spiritual journeys as well as our ongoing research into the system of Reiki.

A big, beautiful thank you to our daughter, Bella, who reminds us of the magic of words as she learns to read a new one every day.

Thanks to Robert Fueston, James Deacon, Colin Powell, Minamida Tokiko, Inamoto Hyakuten, Professor J. Rabinovitch, Nevill Drury, Li Ying, and Chris Marsh for their support and, where necessary, helpful facts and figures.

Thanks Bab Books, Lolly Ellena Rados, the Ittôen community, Sue Paterson, Honda Michiko, and Tony Henderson for illustrations and photos.

And lastly, thank you John Hunt and your team – we appreciate the trust you place in us.

Let us begin by writing:

Mangaichi   ayamariga   arimashitara goyousha kudasai

Please forgive us if we've made a mistake

Introduction

Clarity.

With clarity we can understand what it is we are doing and why. It is the light that brightens our lives and allows us to act with a clear intent and action.

Today there is a strong need for clarity within the system of Reiki. There are so many facts and myths that abound under this term that a sniff of clarity is often experienced as a true blessing.

For this reason the *A-Z of Reiki* focuses the spotlight on a broad range of topics that have touched the system's evolution. They come from both Japan and the West and from its origins to modern day.

Where the spotlight falls is totally individual to the reader. What you find in this book will depend upon your current experience of, and exposure to, the world of Reiki. As your knowledge and understanding grows, you will discover new subjects emerging from between these pages.

Outdated myths may fade away when the spotlight's focus is sharpened upon them, as they should. At other times the light of clarity glances off a diamond's carat so beautifully, it just can't be ignored. These are the many journeys that a reader can traverse in the *A-Z of Reiki*.

Clarity will improve your personal Reiki practice. It will improve your professional Reiki practice. And it will return respect to the system.

The format of the *A-Z of Reiki* is simple. It is like a dictionary or, if you like, an address book. Flip through its alphabetical listing to find out who, or what, you need clarity about.

How to read this book:
Cross references in this book are provided by printing words in bold text. Bold text indicates

that a word is a main-entry. By following through with the cross reference you will find specific information about that particular entry.

Japanese names are written with the surname first as is culturally correct.

The use of upper case is a Western notion and not a Japanese one. When printing Japanese words the authors have taken the liberty of using capitals for people's names and places (in the Western custom) for the reader's added clarity.

The contents of this book are for general information only. If you wish to learn the system of Reiki it is recommended that you find a teacher in your area that can guide you through the teachings and techniques. The authors do not accept any liability for the use or misuse of any practice or technique in this book.

Japanese Pronunciation:

a is similar to the *a* in father
i is similar to the *ea* in eat
u is similar to the *oo* in look
e is similar to the *e* in egg
o is similar to the *o* in go

From *An Introduction to Modern Japanese* by Osamu and Nobuko Mizutani.

Advanced Reiki Training

Sometimes called ART, 3a or **Reiki Master/Practitioner**. It is a Western addition to the system of **Reiki** often practiced in **Usui/Tibetan Reiki** but has also been adopted by many **Independent Reiki Masters**. Some **technique**s taught at this level are crystal grid work, a **healing attunement**, Reiki guide meditation, psychic surgery, **Reiki symbol meditation** and the **antakharana** symbol. Students are taught the **Master Symbol** (**Symbol 4** and/or **Dumo**) but not how to perform the **attunement**.

Aikidô

A form of self-defence martial arts that was founded by **Ueshiba Morihei** who is said to have been an acquaintance of **Usui Mikao**.

Ueshiba Morihei stated that aikidô is a "study of the spirit". It is often called 'The Way of Harmony'.

Alef Reiki

A recently developed practice inspired by the system of **Reiki** that bases itself on the Hebrew Alphabet. No **symbol**s are used and 'Adonai' (God) is invoked for help. USA.

Amanohuna Reiki

A recently developed **non-traditional** practice inspired by the system of **Reiki** where the information is **channel**led and includes 10 **level**s called degrees. It states that Amanohuna is Hawaiian for "Abundance of the Right Way of Life". USA.

Amida Nyorai

This **deity** is taught as the connection to **SHK** and **Symbol 2**. Amida Nyorai is the main deity of **Pure Land** Buddhism. Amida is **Sanskrit**

for Infinite Light. Amida's compassion is therefore also infinite. The main practice of the Pure Land sect is to recite Namu-Amida-Butsu, which is an expression of **Oneness**. Namu-Amida-Butsu translates to, 'I take refuge in Amida Nyorai Buddha'.

Angel

This is an ethereal being that is found in a number of religious traditions including **Judaism**, **Christianity** and **Islam**. An angel's duty is to assist and serve God or the Gods. The concept of angels have been adopted into **New Age movement** beliefs and consequently some recent Western **branch**es **of Reiki**.

Angelic RayKey

A recently developed **non-traditional** practice inspired by the system of **Reiki** which claims to **channel** teachings from **Archangel** St. Michael. USA.

Angel Touch Reiki

A recently developed **non-traditional** practice inspired by the system of **Reiki** and **angel** energy for spiritual transformation. USA.

Animals

Reiki treatments can be performed on

animals.

Hand positions are applied on or near the animal. Often Reiki **first aid** procedures are used where hands are not placed in any specific sequence. In this situation hands are placed directly on the animal's area of complaint.

Animals will clearly indicate to the **Reiki practitioner** if they are accepting of the treatment or not. Animals may show the practitioner that the treatment is finished by moving away.

Anshin Ritsumei

Doi Hiroshi, founder of **Gendai Reiki Hô**, states that **Usui Mikao** "came to recognize that the purpose of life is to attain a state of anshin ritsumei. It means *to learn a fact that man given a roll to play is being sustained by the universe, and to fulfill one's roll with a calm mind by trusting the universe and leaving all to the universe no matter what*

happens in the course of life."
Inamoto Hyakuten, founder of **Komyo Reiki Kai**, states that anshin ritsumei means, "to stay calm and peaceful without any attachment or expectation after having surrendered to the divine will" or simply put, "absolute inner peace".

Antakharana Symbol

 Non-traditional Reiki **symbol**. This symbol has been added to the system of **Reiki** by some Western Reiki teachers including **Arthur Robertson** and is used in **Usui/Tibetan Reiki** as a **meditation technique**. The antakharana is a two dimensional cube with three 7s on its face. Myth has it that this symbol comes from Tibet and China. It is claimed that if you meditate on the antakharana you will connect the physical brain with the **Higher Self**.

Anti-Clockwise Energy Spirals

Non-traditional Western **technique** that

claims to ease the **client** into a change that is about to happen.

Araki, George

He became a **Reiki Master** in 1979. One of **Hawayo Takata**'s 22 Reiki Master students. According to **Robert Fueston**, George Araki initially became a Reiki Master when he was head of the Department of Natural Healing at San Francisco State University and was interested in completing a study about it. He did not teach many people preferring to refer them to either **Fran Brown** or **Shinobu Saito**.

Archangel

High-ranking **angel**. Archangels are found in a number of religious traditions including **Judaism**, **Christianity** and **Islam**. They have been adopted into **New Age movement** beliefs and consequently some recent Western **branch**es **of Reiki**.

Ascended Masters

In the Theosophical teachings of Helena Blavatsky, the Ascended Masters are spiritually enlightened beings such as the Virgin Mary and Muhammad. This element of Theosophy has been included into some recent Western **branches of Reiki**.

Ascension Reiki

A recently developed **non-traditional** practice inspired by the system of **Reiki** which claims to **channel** teachings from the **Ascended Masters**. USA.

Attunement

An attunement is one of the **five elements of the system of Reiki**. There are many different attunement methods as teachers have added to, or taken away from, traditional processes.

The origin of the attunement is the Japanese **reiju** which does not include **symbol**s and/or **mantra**s. There are no limits to the number of reiju one can receive. It is believed that **Hayashi Chûjirô** may have created the basic attunement process that is taught in the West by adding symbols and mantras to the reiju.

The attunement in the West is sometimes known as an **initiation**, **empowerment**, or **transformation**.

The attunement is a **ritual** which supports a teacher of the system to connect strongly with the energy.

Something as profound as an attunement cannot be analyzed on the human level - merely experienced. As an attunement is a powerful clearing of the body's **meridians** it is impossible to be able to undo this or 'wipe-it-out'. Each attunement you receive takes you a step further to moving toward a natural state of balance at all levels; mentally, physically, emotionally and spiritually. For these reasons it is also impossible to 'make' an attunement last for a limited period of time.

Aura

A supernatural energy field around all objects that some claim to be able to see. The aura is said to be linked with the function of the **chakra**s. These concepts have been adopted into **New Age movement** beliefs and consequently some recent Western **branch**es **of Reiki**.

B

Baba, Dorothy

One of **Hawayo Takata**'s 22 **Reiki Master** students who has since passed away. According to **Robert Fueston** she was a social worker who became a Reiki Master around 1976.

Baylow, Ursula (1911-1996)

One of **Hawayo Takata**'s 22 **Reiki Master** students who has since passed away. According to Anneli Twan's book, *Early Days of Reiki-Memories of Hawayo Takata,* Ursula Baylow became a Reiki Master in October 1979.

Beaming

Non-traditional Western **technique** in which **Reiki** is directed to a person/place or thing by turning the palms toward them/it. This technique does not include touch. It is taught in **Usui/Tibetan Reiki** and is practiced by some **Independent Reiki Masters**.

Beggar Story

Most Western **Reiki practitioner**s know the 'beggar story' as a parable told by **Hawayo Takata**. It teaches practitioners that **Reiki** must be paid for or it will not be respected.

Many teachers dispute this concept today and there exist groups of teachers and practitioners who offer **Reiki treatments** and **Reiki courses** for free.

There is an account of the 'beggar story' in *Living Reiki-Takata's Teachings* by **Fran Brown**.

Benefits

Our mind and body know how to heal themselves - the system of **Reiki** supports that innate **healing** process.

One of the most fundamental concepts of Reiki is that the body draws on more energy to clear its **stagnant energy**. This is a non-diagnostic system that accepts that the body draws the energy to where it is most needed.

This system began as a spiritual development practice at the beginning of the 1900s. Once a practitioner feels spiritually whole the physical body follows. By the mid 1920s Usui Mikao began teaching hands-on healing as a form of **first aid** to **naval officers**.

Blockage

Sometimes the word blockage is used to express the lack of movement of energy in a specific area of the body. A more positive view of this experience is that **stagnant energy** is stimulated by working with **Reiki**, resulting in change for the **client**.

Blue Book, The

Paul Mitchell and **Phyllis Lei Furumoto** wrote *The Blue Book–Reiki* in 1985. It includes historical information as taught by **Hawayo**

Takata, some information about **The Reiki Alliance** plus photos of **Usui Mikao**, **Hayashi Chûjirô**, Hawayo Takata and Phyllis Lei Furumoto.

Bockner, Rick

One of **Hawayo Takata**'s 22 **Reiki Master**s. According to **Robert Fueston** he became a Reiki Master on 12 October 1980 at **Bethal Phaigh**'s house in Slocan Valley. He completed **Level I** on 10 October 1979 and his **Level II** on 20 October 1979. Robert Fueston also notes that, according to **Wanja Twan**, Rick Bockner was also the last Reiki Master to be taught by Hawayo Takata. He is currently a member of **The Reiki Alliance**.

Brahma Satya Reiki

A recently developed **non-traditional** practice inspired by the system of **Reiki** which claims to **channel** teachings from a Master. India.

Branch of Reiki

The system of **Reiki** began in the early 1900s. Since the death of its founder **Usui Mikao**, a number of different branches of the system have developed in Japan.

Since 1980, a great variety of Reiki branches and teachings inspired by the system of Reiki have also been created in the West. This has lead to many individual teachings which may or may not relate to what was once taught by Usui Mikao in Japan.

Over the last thirty years the system of Reiki has been a leader in the popularity of energy **healing** in the West. Its structure of three **level**s with its interesting mix of self-help and mysticism has been replicated many times over with slight variations. This has meant the actual word 'Reiki' has been adopted for use in systems and practices unrelated to the system of Reiki. To find out the minimum requirements for a Reiki branch see **Five Elements of the System of Reiki**.

Within the *A-Z of Reiki* a number of branches are listed. Some are major branches while others are relatively unknown. Some are simply inspired by the system of Reiki rather than directly related to it. This is in order to give a cross section of what is happening within the system today.

Breath of the Fire Dragon

Non-traditional breath **technique** used with an **attunement** process. Variations of this are the blue kidney breath, Reiki breathing and **violet breath**. It was originally taught in **Raku Kei Reiki**.

Brown, Barbara (1915?-2000)

One of **Hawayo Takata**'s 22 **Reiki Master**s. Anneli Twan's book, *Early Days of Reiki-Memories of Hawayo Takata*, states that Barbara Brown became a Reiki Master on 12 October 1979 in Cherryville, BC, Canada along with **Wanja Twan** and **Bethal Phaigh**. The inaugural **Reiki Alliance** meeting was held at Barbara Brown's house in British Columbia in 1983. She passed away on Easter Sunday, 2000 and was in her mid-80s.

Brown, Fran

One of **Hawayo Takata**'s 22 **Reiki Masters**. According to **Robert Fueston** she is the seventh Reiki Master trained by Hawayo Takata. She completed **Level I** on 3 June 1973 with Hawayo Takata. She then took her **Level II** training from **John Gray** in 1976. She became a Reiki Master on 15 January 1979 in Keosauqua, Iowa. She is a member of **The Reiki Alliance** and has published a book entitled *Living Reiki-Takata's Teachings*. Though she is in her late 70s she continues to teach all over the world, including Japan.

Buddhism

A Japanese form of Buddhism called **Tendai** is said to have been a large influence on the

teachings of **Usui Mikao**. **Suzuki san** claims
that he was a Tendai lay priest.

In the 1980s and 90s other forms of Buddhism
such as Tibetan Buddhism were claimed to
lie at the foundation of the system of
Reiki. This is unlikely however as Buddhism
originated in India and moved to China and
Tibet independent of each other. Chinese
Buddhism travelled across to Japan from the
seventh century and over the last 1400 years
has developed its own unique Japanese form.

Japanese esoteric Buddhism is a term that
includes **Mikkyô** and **Shugendô** practices.
Within these forms esoteric rituals involving
mantras, **mudra**s, and mandalas are used.

Buddho Symbol

Non-traditional symbol utilized in
Reiki Jin Kei do. Claimed to be a
'Tibetan' **symbol** handed down by
Buddha and is used with **med-
itation**. This **lineage** has not been verified

though claims a non-**Takata** lineage.

C

Budô

Refers to the traditional art of self-defence in Japan. Some different kinds of budo are **jûdô**, karate, **aikidô**, kendô, and iaidô. It is claimed that **Usui Mikao** studied martial arts and gained **menkyo kaiden**, the highest license of proficiency.

Byôsen Reikan Hô

(Japanese) Sense imbalances in the body.

Traditional Japanese **technique** similar to the Western technique of **scanning**.

C

Certificate

Certification is often given to students at the end of a **Reiki course**. There is no one true form of Reiki certification. Included here is a

Reiki certificate from the Japanese **Reiki** C **Master**, **Inamoto Hyakuten**.

In the West a certificate signifies that a student has simply completed whatever it is that the **Reiki Master** teaches. There are no across the board standards. It is possible to finish **Levels I**, **II**, or even **III** in a weekend. This leaves the student feeling temporarily powerful without actually becoming empowered. When an individual receives **attunement**s over a couple of days the body's energy cannot differentiate between having received a Level I, II, or III certificate.

Reiki is not about certification - it is about personal practice. In traditional Japanese teachings a certificate is given to indicate that certain levels of proficiency have been reached and that the student is just beginning that actual **level**.

Chakra
Chakra is a **Sanskrit** word often translated as

'wheel of energy'. There are a minimum of 7 major chakras in the body. Chakras, though Indian in origin, are popularly used in many **New Age movement** forms of energetic work. They've also recently been included in some modern forms of the system of **Reiki**.

There is no record of **Usui Mikao**, or his students **Eguchi Toshihiro**, **Tomita Kaiji** or **Hayashi Chûjirô** working with chakras.

Hawayo Takata wrote of the "true energy" in the body that "lies in the bottom of the stomach about 2 inches below the navel" in **The Gray Book** where **Alice Takata Furumoto** had compiled information from her diary notes. Here Hawayo Takata is referring to the **hara** energetic method that is used in Japan.

Chakras have been taught in the system of Reiki by a number of Hawayo Takata's students including **John Harvey Gray** and **Iris Ishikuro**. **Barbara Weber Ray** also bases The **Radiance Technique** on the chakra system. In some Western **branches of Reiki** it is claimed that an **attunement** clears or opens a particular C chakra. This is, however, a modern interpretation of the system.

Chakra Balancing
Non-traditional Western **technique** to balance the **chakra**s with one another. Taught in **Satya Reiki**.

Chakra Kassei Kokyû Hô
Non-traditional Western breathing **technique** to activate the **chakra**s.

Channel (1)
It is said that a **Reiki practitioner** 'channels' **Reiki**. What is being described here is the practitioner's act of stimulating Reiki to move through the body. A practitioner does this by practicing **technique**s to strengthen his/her energy, by receiving **reiju** or **attunement**s, and by focusing with a clear **intent**.

Channel (2)

Another meaning of channel is to do with mediumship and communicating with those who have passed away or exist in another dimension. Some recent **branch**es **of Reiki** aligned with **New Age movement** beliefs claim to channel information from sources that are no longer alive.

Chanting

A **technique** that uses the voice to stimulate energy. The chanting of **mantra**s is taught in a variety of ways in the system of **Reiki**.

Chiba

The name of **Usui Mikao**'s ancestors. The Chiba clan was one of the most famous and influential samurai families in all of Japan according to the Chiba family records. The Usui **memorial stone** states that the famous samurai, **Chiba Tsunetane** (1118– 1201) was Usui Mikao's ancestor. This may be incorrect as

C

Doi Hiroshi states it was the samurai **Chiba Toshitane** instead.

The Usui family crest, otherwise known as the Chiba **mon** which is shown here, is a design comprising the moon and a star. These were also the symbols of Myoken Bodhisattva. Myoken was once an icon for the **samurai**.

Chiba Toshitane

A famous **samurai** warlord from the 1500s. In 1551 he conquered the city Usui and thereafter all family members acquired that name.

The memorial stones states that the famous samurai, **Chiba Tsunetane** (1118– 1201), was **Usui Mikao**'s ancestor. **Doi Hiroshi** notes that this was incorrect and that it was in fact Chiba Toshitane.

Chiba Tsunetane (1118–1201)

The **memorial stone** states that the famous

samurai, Chiba Tsunetane, was **Usui Mikao**'s ancestor.

Chi Ka So

Non-traditional symbol taught at the 5th level of **Barbara Weber Ray**'s **The Radiance Technique**. It is associated with the throat **chakra**.

Chiryô Hô

(Japanese) Treatment.

This term is used in the description of a number of Japanese Reiki **technique**s.

Cho Ku Ret

Non-traditional symbol taught in **Seichim**.

Christianity

The system of **Reiki** is not a religion and is used by people of all religions around the world. Many Christians, including some nuns and priests, practice the system of **Reiki** on themselves and others.

CKR

As the traditional **mantra**s of the system of **Reiki** are considered as **sacred** by many, pseudonyms are used in the *A-Z of Reiki* rather than the true mantras. The pseudonym for the first **traditional** mantra is the initials CKR.

The main Western characteristic of CKR is **Power** and it is spoken three times in conjunction with **Symbol 1**.

The main Japanese characteristic is **Focus**. In Japan, the mantra is not necessarily used in conjunction with the **symbol**. The early teachings of **Usui Mikao** claim that CKR develops a **Reiki practitioner**'s link to the energy of **Earth**.

CKR is a Japanese mantra (**jumon**) that is not only found in the teachings of Usui Mikao. It is also used within the **Oomoto** religion. An interesting point however is that Oomoto appears to have taken it from **Shintô** teachings.

A spokesman for Oomoto, Masamichi Tanaka, wrote that the true mantra (not the pseudonym) of CKR literally means "Direct Spirit" and that it is a part of the Divine Spirit which all of us are bestowed with from God, the Creator of the universe. He went on to write that, "This is a word (or term) we use at Oomoto and Shintô."

Goi Masahisa (1916-1980) founder of the Japanese **new religion** Byakkô Shinkôkai also wrote that the meaning of the true mantra (not the pseudonym) CKR in his religion was "direct spirits".

One more interesting point is that Oomoto and Byakkô Shinkôkai appear to have no concern with writing about or discussing the true mantra with those outside their religion, unlike some in the system of Reiki (hence the need for pseudonyms in the *A-Z of Reiki*). Reiki practitioners can learn from this Japanese attitude to symbols and mantras to overcome

what may be exaggerated Western mysticism. [C]
This Japanese perspective also supports the
understanding that it is not the mantra or
symbol that is 'powerful' but rather the strength
of the practitioner's commitment to practice.

Cleansing

With any form of natural healing method there
exists a cleansing. This may happen during or
immediately after a **Reiki treatment**, or within
a few days.

During a treatment the **client**'s body draws
in energy. It washes through, clearing the body
out on a physical, mental, emotional and/or
spiritual level. This cleansing may be obvious
or very subtle and is sometimes called a
clearing or a **healing crisis**. See also **Three-
Week Cleansing Process**.

Clearing

See **Cleansing**.

Client

A person who receives a **Reiki treatment** from a **Reiki practitioner**. A Reiki client is not referred to as a patient as this would indicate that the client was sick, which is not necessarily the case. Using the word patient is also suggestive of a quasi-medical environment that may inappropriately represent the treatment as diagnostic.

Communicating with Your Higher Self

Non-traditional technique where one re-connects with the **Higher Self**.

Connection

In some Japanese teachings this word is used to describe the characteristic of **HSZSN** and **Symbol 3**. This **mantra** and **symbol** help one remember that a connection between everything already exists. This stimulates **Oneness** between the **Reiki practitioner** and

client. If a practitioner becomes One with everything it becomes unnecessary to 'send' **Reiki** to someone or something.

The symbol itself is Japanese **kanji** meaning 'my original nature is a correct thought' or another translation taught by **Doi Hiroshi** is 'right consciousness is the origin of everything'.

Crystal Healing

Crystals are renowned as excellent **healer**s. There are now many versions of crystal healing being used in Western **branch**es **of Reiki**.

D

Dainichi Nyorai

Symbol 4 helps practitioners connect to this **deity**. Dainichi Nyorai is the Great Shining Buddha because this Buddha is the 'Life force of the Buddhas that Illuminate Everything'. Dainichi dispels the darkness of the world by casting light everywhere, giving life to and nurturing all living things. The wrathfull face of Dainichi Nyorai is **Fudô Myôô**.

Daiseishi Bosatsu

Symbol 1 helps practitioners connect to this **deity**. The name means 'He who Proceeds with Great Vigour'.

Darani

(Japanese) A spell.

From the 13th century in Japan, it was

thought that **waka** achieved supernatural effects because they were darani or spells. **Usui Mikao** included in his teachings 125 waka penned by the **Meiji Emperor**.

D

Degree

Another name for the word 'level' used within the system of **Reiki**.

Deity

God or Goddess.

Den

(Japanese) Legend, tradition and teachings.

In some Japanese branches of Reiki the name of the **level**s ends with – den, for example **Shoden** (first teachings). This system originates from Japanese martial arts.

Denju

(Japanese) Handing down of the teachings.

This Japanese Buddhist term has recently

been adopted by some **Reiki practitioner**s to replace the word **reiju**. Denju could be interpreted to mean reiju but may more accurately indicate the entire teachings. See **Buddhism**.

De-programming Techniques

There are two traditional Japanese **technique**s that work on releasing set mental patterns. One is **nentatsu hô** and the other is **seiheki chiryô hô**. In the West, a number of variations of these techniques are practiced.

Distance Symbol

The name is sometimes applied to **HSZSN** and **Symbol 3** in Western forms of the system of **Reiki**. The **mantra** and **symbol** are commonly used for **distant healing**. According to the Western system of Reiki they create a bridge between the sender and receiver.

In Japan, the characteristic of the mantra and symbol is considered to be **Connection**.

Distant Attunement

Attunements in the West were initially [D] performed in person but in the event of globalization, attunements are now being sent by distance. This method is an extension of the concept of **distant healing**, which has been used in both Western and Japanese systems of **Reiki**.

Distant Healing

Distant healing is used to send **Reiki** for the purpose of **healing** to someone who is not physically present. **Symbol 3** is said to activate this **technique** and is taught at **Level II**. In the West, numerous techniques are used in conjunction with distant healing including the **photo technique** and **healing lists**. The related Japanese technique is called **enkaku chiryô hô**.

Distant Reiki

Send **Reiki** to a person, place or thing in the past, present or future with **distant healing**.

DKM

As the traditional **mantra**s of the system of **Reiki** are considered as **sacred** by many, pseudonyms are used in the *A-Z of Reiki* rather than the true mantras. The pseudonym for the fourth **traditional** mantra is the initials DKM.

The kanji of the true mantra of DKM is actually **Symbol 4**.

The main Western characteristic of DKM is as the **Master Symbol** and it is spoken three times in conjunction with Symbol 4.

The main Japanese characteristic is **Empowerment**. In Japan, the mantra is not necessarily used in conjunction with the symbol. The early teachings of **Usui Mikao** claim that DKM develops a **Reiki practitioner**'s true nature.

This mantra is not used only within Usui Mikao's teachings. It can be found in some Japanese martial arts as well as in **Mikkyô**, **Shugendô**, and some of the **new religions** like Shunmei.

Dô

(Japanese) Way or method.

A term commonly used in Japan to describe a teacher's method, like **aikidô** and **jûdô**.

Doctor

Usui Mikao was given the title 'Doctor' by a Western **Reiki** student, **Hawayo Takata**. This lead to some believing that he was actually a physician even thought it was not the case.

Using this type of terminolgy can be seen as misleading for **client**s and students – leading them to believe that the system of Reiki's origins were allopathic. Constant repetition of this mis-information does not promote the system of Reiki as a reputable practice.

However, his student **Hayashi Chûjirô** *was* a doctor and his medical background is claimed to have helped Usui Mikao create the **Usui Reiki Ryôhô Gakkai**'s healing guide.

Doi Hiroshi

Teacher of **Gendai Reiki Hô**. Doi Hiroshi was one of the first Japanese to study **Levels** I and II in Japan with **Mieko Mitsui** a **Radiance Technique** teacher. He also studied Osho Neo Reiki to the teacher level and is an **Okuden** member of the **Usui Reiki Ryôhô Gakkai**.

Dôjô

(Japanese) A place of the path.

Generally speaking a place where we learn something. This term is most often used in martial arts like **jûdô**, karate, kendô, etc. On **Usui Mikao**'s **memorial stone** it states that he set up a dôjô at Nakano in Tôkyô.

Dumo

Non-traditional symbols introduced to the

system of **Reiki** in the West. There are two symbols with the one name. Dumo is sometimes called the Tibetan Master **symbol** and is taught in **Usui/Tibetan Reiki.**

It is claimed to be a 'modern-day **Symbol 4**'. Those who teach this believe that the energy today is different to that of **Usui Mikao**'s time. Even if this were true the traditional Symbol 4 has specific meanings which have no correlation to the Dumo symbol.

E

Earth

In Japan, Earth is often described as one half of the universe with **Heaven** being its opposite force. An ancient Japanese cosmological theory states that through the union of these dual forces all things were born. In **Usui Mikao**'s early teachings the **CKR** and **Symbol 1** are said to be associated with the energy of the Earth: heavy, powerful and grounding.

Doi Hiroshi has stated, "In the Gakkai the words 'harmony of Ten-Chi-Jin' and 'Oneness of Great Universe (the macrocosm) and Small Universe (humans or the microcosm)' are often used." Ten is Heaven, Chi is Earth, and Jin is humans. See also **In and Yô**.

Eguchi Toshihiro (1873 – 1946)

Professor J. Rabinovitch has been collecting

research about Eguchi Toshihiro from material that includes his diaries and monographs and states that he was both a student and long-time friend of **Usui Mikao**. According to a recently published Japanese book by Mihashi Kazuo on Eguchi Toshihiro's life *Tenohira-ga Byoki-o Naosu*, he was born in Kumamoto, studied at Tokyo University, and was the Principal of a junior high school. He also wrote **waka**.

E

As his health had never been very good, as an older man he claimed that only two good things had happened in his life; that he had started practicing **hands-on healing** and found a good husband for his wife. His wife's husband was **Miyazaki Gorô**, a hands-on healing student of Eguchi Toshihiro.

Due to Eguchi Toshihiro's popularity as a teacher of hands-on healing he is most likely to have influenced many hands-on healing teachings at that time.

Eguchi Toshihiro created the **Tenohira** Ryôji Kenkyû Kai (Hand Healing Research Center) in 1928 and wrote a number of books: *Te No Hira Ryôji Nyûmon (Introduction to Healing with the Palms)* in 1930 and *Te No Hira Ryôji Wo Kataru (A Story of Healing with the Palms)* in 1954. **Doi Hiroshi** states that Eguchi Toshihiro studied Usui Mikao's teachings between 1925 and 1927.

Eguchi Toshihiro was a member of the **Usui Reiki Ryôhô Gakkai** for two years but, according to Mihashi Kazuo, he apparently found the 50 yen admission fee to be too expensive. At that time **Taketomi Kanichi** was teaching and as he was a financially well-off **naval officer** Eguchi Toshihiro could not understand why such large sums of money were required. At every meeting members were also asked to pay 1 yen. Eventually Eguchi Toshihiro wrote a letter to the Usui Reiki Ryôhô Gakkai president, **Ushida Jûzaburô**, resigning from the society.

In this photo Eguchi Toshihiro is performing his own form of **reiju** called kosho michibiki

(illuminating guidance) from his teachings. This is known to have taken place in a group format and may have been performed individually.

According to Mihashi Kazuo, he also taught specific **hand positions**, **meditation**, the recitation of the **Meiji Emperor**'s waka by students on a daily basis, and principles for an ascetic life.

In 1929, he taught members of the **Ittôen** community his system, with some families still practicing these hands-on healing practices today. Professor J. Rabinovitch states that,

"Ittôen folks have told me that there were no **level**s, no formal rituals or **attunement**s in Eguchi's way of doing things."

His teachings became very popular with about 150 to 300 people in attendance. A book by his student **Mitsui Kôshi** about the teachings increased this popularity. He even travelled to Pusan in Korea to teach. **Mochizuki Toshitaka** states in his book that Eguchi Toshihiro taught approximately 500,000 students. This large number may include all students who have studied his teachings over the years.

According to **Suzuki san** it was Eguchi Toshihiro who was responsible for adding the 3 **mantra**s/**jumon** into **Level II** of the system of Reiki.

Professor J. Rabinovitch also wrote this about Eguchi Toshihiro, "One important thing to bear in mind is that Eguchi did not have many 'methods' of the modern sort to speak of and in his writing plainly states that people

with methods start to rely on those as though
it is the 'method' that leads to healing, when
it is other deeper spiritual connections that
bring **healing**."

Empowerment (1)

This word is often used to describe the Japanese
reiju and/or the Western **attunement** process.

Empowerment (2)

In some Japanese teachings this word is used to
describe the characteristics of **DKM** and
Symbol 4.

Energy Exchange

Although the concept of energy exchange is
innate in human nature, this term is utilised
in Western forms of Reiki to ensure students
take responsibility for their own health. The
client is asked to return the favour of a **Reiki
treatment** by doing 'something' for the **Reiki
practitioner**. In this way the client is more

respectful of the treatment, leaving him/her with a sense of self-responsibility for his/her own health. See **Money**.

Enjudô

(Japanese) A hall where one's life is lengthened.

This is a specific hall within a Japanese monastery where monks and nuns perform **healing**. This healing can take place on either a physical or spiritual level.

Enkaku Chiryô Hô

(Japanese) Remote **healing**.

This practice is related to the Western **technique** called **distant healing**.

En-no-Gyoja

(Japanese) The ascetic En.

The legendary founder of **Shugendô** also known as En-no-Ozunu (see photo). He is said to have been born in 634. From the age of 32 he practiced esoteric **Buddhism** and laid the foundations for Shugendô (esoteric mountain Buddhism).

E

Researchers today claim that **Usui Mikao** practised Shugendô and that many of the understandings of the system of **Reiki** grew from it.

Due to the outlawing of Shugendô in 1872, the author of *Shugendô*, Miyake Hitoshi, wrote that many **new religions** sprang up "to take its place and respond to the human need for fulfilling worldly aspirations." Shugendô thus became the central foundation for many of these new religions. Reiki is not a religion. It was created as a system that could be openly practiced by individuals regardless of their beliefs. It does however have similar origins to many of the new religions of that particular time in Japanese history.

Enryaku Ji

Main **Tendai** temple on **hiei zan**, near Kyôto, Japan. There are claims that **Usui Mikao** trained and studied here and that old **sutra** copies at enryaku ji still bear his Buddhist name. Included is a photo of monks at enryaku ji.

Ewing, Patricia

One of the 22 **Reiki Master** students trained by **Hawayo Takata**.

F

Facet

A variation of the word 'level' used by some **branches of Reiki** e.g. Facet 2 instead of **Level II**.

Finishing Treatment

A blood cleansing **technique** that is also called the **nerve stroke**. In Japan, traditional versions of this are **zenshin kôketsu hô**, **hanshin kôketsu hô**, and **ketsueki kôkan hô**. **Hawayo Takata** taught this technique at **Level II**.

Fire Serpent

Non-traditional symbol used in many Tibetan **branches of Reiki**. Also called Nin Gizzida, Serpent Raku or Tibetan Fire Serpent. The Fire Serpent **symbol**

is drawn with a horizontal line across the top of the student's crown, snaking down the spine, and spiraling clockwise at the base of the spine thus claiming to ground energy into the lower body. It is also claimed to be of use in **healing**, **meditation** or **attunement**s to promote balance and receptivity.

First Aid

In the mid-1920s **Usui Mikao** taught **hands-on healing** to a group of **naval officers**. The intention was that while at sea they would be able to work energetically on themselves and others, especially in first aid situations. This group were the founding members of a society that still exists in Japan today called the **Usui Reiki Ryôhô Gakkai**.

To use Reiki as a form of first aid immediately place the hands on or near the area of need.

Five Elements of the System of Reiki

No matter what the background, all **Reiki** branches should have a minimum of five elements in common. These elements are all **ritual**s that are created to help **Reiki practitioner**s develop structure and routine. The five elements are that every student receives **attunements** or **reiju**, and learns about **hand position**s, the **precepts**, **symbol**s and **mantras** (from **Level II** onward), and **meditation**s and/or **technique**s.

Five Head Positions

A number of **hand positions** on the head are included in the *Reiki Ryôhô Hikkei* and **Hayashi Chûjirô**'s *Ryôhô Shishin*.

Five similar head positions below are claimed by **Suzuki san** to have been taught by **Usui Mikao**.

They are:

zentô bu – forehead

sokutô bu – both temples

kôtô bu – back of your head and forehead

enzui bu – either side of neck

tôchô bu – crown on top of head

Eguchi Toshihiro, a well-known hands-on **healer** and friend of Usui Mikao, used a similar set of hand positions in his manuals and added one last position at the stomach. Following is a translation of his five head positions taken from his joint publication with **Mitsui Kôshi** in 1930. The positions are:

haegiwa – hairline

komekami – temples 'you can do both sides with both hands at once'

kôtôbu no takai tokoro – rear of head, high up

kubisuji - nape of neck

atama no chôjô – top of head (crown)

ichoo - stomach, intestines

Five Precepts

For today only: Do not anger; Do not worry; Be humble; Be honest in your work; and Be compassionate to yourself and others.

These precepts are the cornerstone of **Usui Mikao**'s teachings and are guidelines to aid students in their spiritual development journey. The **Usui Reiki Ryôhô Gakkai** perform **gokai sansho** (chanting of the five precepts three times) at the end of their regular group meetings called **kenkyû kai**.

The precepts are spiritual teachings rather than religious teachings and students are asked to consider them in their daily actions. They are also a part of the **ritual**ism of the system of **Reiki**. The words are used to connect **Reiki practitioner**s to certain thoughts in order to help move energy. Without these initial words and their intentions, practitioners would not know where to begin. After much personal work using these precepts it is possible to tap into their energy without the words themselves. This occurs when the practitioner is totally in the flow of his or her practice.

Recently, it has been asserted that the origins of the five precepts actually date back to ninth century Japanese Buddhist precepts. The original Japanese version of the precepts (translated at the beginning of this entry) above originate from the Usui Reiki Ryôhô Gakkai and may have been developed to suit the Usui Reiki Ryôhô Gakkai's first members, the Japanese **naval officers**.

The Japanese version shown here is apparently not in Usui Mikao's handwriting according to **Doi Hiroshi** and **Inamoto Hyakuten**.

F

Focus

In some Japanese teachings this word is used to describe the characteristics of **CKR** and **Symbol 1**.

Fudô Myôô

Fudô Myôô is the wrathful face of **Dainichi Nyorai**. Fudô Myôô is often depicted with flames (to consume passions), a sword in his right hand (to conquer and cut through ignorance, greed, anger and injustice), and a rope in his left hand (to bind demons). In esoteric Japanese **Buddhism** Fudô Myôô is connected to the **mantra** taught at **Level III** of the system of **Reiki**.

Fueston, Robert

Reiki researcher who focuses mainly on **Hawayo Takata**, her teachings, and her students. Robert Fueston has trained with some of Hawayo Takata's Master students as well as Japanese teachers like **Doi Hiroshi** and **Inamoto Hyakuten**.

Funakoshi Gichin (1868–1957)

Founder of modern karate. He is said to have known **Usui Mikao**. **Shinpei Goto** knew both Funakoshi Gichin (he wrote a calligraphic work for Funakoshi Gichin's first book in 1922) and Usui Mikao. In 1922 Usui Mikao moved his seat of learning to Tôkyô where Funakoshi Gichin taught and Shinpei Goto lived.

Furumoto, Alice Takata

The daughter of **Hawayo Takata** and the mother of **Phyllis Lei Furumoto**. Alice Takata Furumoto compiled *The Gray Book* (called

Leiki), which was handed out to some of Hawayo Takata's Master students.

Furumoto, Phyllis Lei

The granddaughter of **Hawayo Takata**. She became a **Reiki Master** in April of 1979 in Keosauqua, Iowa and is a trained psychologist.

Phyllis Lei Furumoto is said to have apprenticed with her grandmother for the year and a half before she passed on.

She is also a founding member of **The Reiki Alliance**. The Reiki Alliance state they have honoured her with their 'title of holder' of the 'Office of the **Grandmaster**' and also called her the **lineage** bearer of the system of **Reiki**.

In 1992, Phyllis Lei Furumoto resigned as a member though retained her official title. In 2004 she rejoined The Reiki Alliance.

Futomani Divination Chart

The Futomani Divination Chart stems from

the **Hotsuma Tsutae**. Copies of the *Hotsuma Tsutae* have been stored in iwamuro (cave storage) in a **Tendai** temple at **enryaku ji**

(**hiei zan**, Kyôto). These copies were given to Saichô (767–822), the founding priest of enryaku ji. The origin of this text is controversial. Tendai priests were believed to give lectures on the *Hotsuma Tsutae*. The divination chart has 48 syllables attributed to deities that form the matrix of magic signs. One of the letterforms in the divination chart, the 'wa', resembles the essence of **Symbol 1**.

F

G

Gasshô

(Japanese) To place the two palms together.

This is a Japanese gesture of respect, gratitude, veneration and humility. This simple act balances both the mind and body. There are many varieties of gasshô.

Gasshô Kokyû Hô

(Japanese) Gasshô breathing **technique**.

Also called **seishin toitsu** and is part of the **technique hatsurei hô**.

Gasshô Meditation

A **meditation technique** where one concentrates on the hands.

Gateway Symbol

G

Non-traditional symbol taught at the 7th **level** of the **Seven Level System**, com-
monly known as the infinity **symbol**. Claims to activate a **chakra** called the gateway chakra where the neck meets the back of the skull.

Gedoku Hô

A similar **technique** to **tanden chiryô hô**. One hand is placed on the front of the **hara** and the other hand on the back of the hara. This technique is listed in the *shiori* for **Usui Reiki Ryôhô Gakkai** members.

Gendai Reiki Hô

A new **Reiki** method developed by **Doi Hiroshi**. It is a fusion between **Usui Mikao**'s philosophy and the rationality of Western forms of Reiki. It teaches a mixture of **traditional** and **non-traditional techniques** Japan.

Gnosa Symbol

Non-traditional symbol used in **Karuna Reiki®**, **Tera Mai™**, and **Karuna Ki**. It is said to connect the higher self with lower self, increase creativity, and improve learning abilities and communication.

Gokai

(Japanese) **Five precepts**.

Gokai No Sho

(Japanese) Book of **five precepts**.

This is a calligraphic scroll of the five **Reiki** precepts and is entitled '**Usui Mikao Sensei** Ikun **Gokai**' (The Five Precepts, an admonition of the late Usui Mikao).

Yamaguchi Chiyoko had such a work,

brushstroked by her teacher, **Hayashi Chûjirô**. Although Hayashi Chûjirô created his own school he still showed his respect for the teachings of Usui Mikao by teaching classes in front of this scroll.

G

Gokai Sansho

(Japanese) To sing the **five precepts** three times.

This is a **Buddhist** term. It is still practiced by the **Usui Reiki Ryôhô Gakkai** at the end of their meetings.

Gokui Kaiden

(Japanese) Ultimate stage of proficiency.

Teacher level in **Gendai Reiki Hô**, **Doi Hiroshi**'s **branch of Reiki**.

Go Shimbô

(Japanese) Patience, endurance or perseverance.

This is a **Tendai ritual** that has similarities

to the **reiju** and is known as 'Dharma for
Protecting the Body'. Sometimes written as Go
Shinbô.

Goto Shinpei (1857–1929)

After studying at medical school he worked in
various important Government positions. He
became well known for advocating philan-
thropy and the principle of a 'Large Family'
when he took the position of Governor of the
Standard of Railways. After the Kanto earth-
quake in September 1923, he played an active
role in rebuilding Tokyô. As a politician his
nickname was 'Big Talker'. Shinpei Goto
became the Mayor of Tokyô in 1920 and it has
been said that **Usui Mikao** had worked for him.
Shinpei Goto wrote a calligraphic work in
Funakoshi Gichin's first book in 1922 called
Ryukyu Kempo: Tode. Funakoshi Gichin is also
said to have been an acquaintance of Usui
Mikao. In 1924, Citizen's forerunner, the
Shokosha Watch Research Institute produced

its first pocket watch. Shinpei Goto named the watch CITIZEN with the hope that the watch (a luxury item) would become widely available to ordinary citizens and be sold throughout the world.

G

Grandmaster

The term Grandmaster was never used by **Usui Mikao** or **Hayashi Chûjirô**.

It was introduced in the early 1980s by **The Reiki Alliance**. **Phyllis Lei Furumoto**, **Hawayo Takata**'s granddaughter, received the title 'Office of the Grandmaster' from this organization.

Today some teachers of Reiki have self-nominated themselves as grandmasters or even great-grandmasters. It is generally accepted that this is a marketing ploy rather than having anything to do with the system of **Reiki**.

Gray, Reverend Beth

Beth Gray completed **Levels I** and **II** with **Hawayo Takata**. Her then husband, **John Harvey Gray**, became a **Reiki Master** with Hawayo Takata in 1976.

In 1976, Beth Gray ordained Hawayo Takata as a minister on the basis of the spiritual nature of her teachings.

According to **Robert Fueston**, John Harvey Gray 'initiated' Beth Gray as a Reiki Master in October 1979 while Hawayo Takata was alive even though it is believed she had asked that her students should not initiate any Reiki Masters until she died.

Hawayo Takata, however is known to have treated her as a teacher and her name is included in the list of 22 Reiki Masters that Hawayo Takata had left with her sister.

Robert Fueston also states that Beth Gray founded the first and largest Usui Shiki Ryôhô Reiki center in the United States. She no longer practices after experiencing a stroke in 1993.

Gray Book, The

Also called the *Leiki* booklet by some. **Alice Takata Furumoto** compiled this booklet in 1982. It includes notes and photographs of **Hawayo Takata**, a copy of Hawayo Takata's **certificate** signed by **Hayashi Chûjirô**, a list of Hawayo Takata's teacher students and the *Ryôhô Shishin* (*Healing Guide*). Hayashi Chûjirô wrote this guide especially for American Distribution. It shows **hand positions** for treating specific illnesses.

G

Gray, John Harvey

One of **Hawayo Takata**'s 22 **Reiki Master** students. He was initiated on 6 October 1976 in Woodside, California. He was the third Reiki Master initiated by Hawayo Takata. He was once married to **Beth Gray** but has since remarried. He is the author of *Hand to Hand-The Longest-Practicing Reiki Master Tells His Story*, published in 2002.

Grounding

A **technique** to reconnect to the center of the **Earth** energetically. An excellent practice for those who work solely with their intuitive skills and find that they are feeling regularly ungrounded.

Group Distant Healing

A **technique** where a group of **Reiki practitioner**s send **Reiki** to someone or something not present.

Group Reiki

Working with **Reiki** in a group environment. A number of **Reiki practitioner**s place their hands on or near the **client** at the same time to support the client's healing process. Based on a traditional Japanese technique called **shûchû Reiki**.

Gyoho (Gyotse)

Claimed by some to be **Usui Mikao**'s Buddhist

name. This name is written on the **memorial stone** in Tôkyô.

It has been claimed that there are copies of old **sutra**s with Usui Mikao's Buddhist name on it at **hiei zan**.

G

Others claim that Gyoho was either a pen name or extra name.

Gyosei

(Japanese) **Waka** written by the **Emperor**.

It is said that the **Meiji Emperor** had written over 100,000 waka and his Empress Shoken over 30,000.

Usui Mikao taught over 100 gyosei according to the **Usui Reiki Ryôhô Gakkai** to support spiritual development.

The Usui Reiki Ryôhô Gakkai recite gyosei at the beginning of their meetings (**kenkyû kai**).

Tomita Kaiji, a student of Usui Mikao, writes in his 1933 book *Reiki To Jinjutsu–Tomita Ryû Teate Ryôhô* (*Reiki and*

Humanitarian Work–Tomita Ryû Hands Healing) that **hatsurei hô** is a **meditation** using gyosei.

Eguchi Toshihiro also taught gyosei in his teachings according to the author Mihashi Kazuo.

Gyôshi Hô
(Japanese) **Healing** by staring **technique**.

Gyôsho
(Japanese) **Kanji** drawn in a modern, semi cursive style.

A simplification of the standard style of writing kanji, allowing it to be written in a more flowing and faster manner.

H

Hadô Kokyû Hô
(Japanese) Vibrational breathing **technique**.

Hadô Meiso Hô
(Japanese) Vibrational **meditation technique**.

Halu Symbol

Non-traditional symbol used in **Karuna Reiki®**, **Tera Mai™**, and **Karuna Ki**. It is said to heal unconscious patterns, the shadow, sexual and physical abuse issues and works on **psychic attack**. This was the third of a number of **channel**ed **symbols** that were claimed to be retrieved by a 'Very High Being' from the Inner Planes and given to Kathleen Milner and Marcy Miller from the USA.

Hand Positions

Hand positions refer to the specific hand positions that are used when performing a **Reiki treatment**. In this photo a Reiki treatment is being offered and received. It is taken from **Tomita Kaiji**'s book published in 1933; he was a student of **Usui Mikao**. **Reiki practitioner**s place their hands on specific body regions with the intention of assisting the energy to move through the body. The purpose is to clear and strengthen the **client**'s spiritual and energetic connection.

A one-hour Reiki treatment consists of a practitioner placing hands on or near the body of the client. Hand positions are also taught to be used by the practitioner for **self-healing**.

It is claimed that in **Usui Mikao**'s early teachings only **five head positions** were used. **Professor J. Rabinovitch** has translated a book by **Eguchi Toshihiro** (a friend and student of Usui Mikao) co-written with his student **Mitsui Kôshi** in 1930, and it shows a similar set of five hand positions for the head.

A number of head positions are written up in related healing guides such as the *Ryôhô Shishin* by **Hayashi Chûjirô** and in the **Usui Reiki Ryôhô Gakkai**'s manual called the *Reiki Ryôhô Hikkei*. In this latter manual Usui Mikao is quoted as saying, "My method is beyond a modern science so you do not need knowledge of medicine. If brain disease occurs, I treat a head. If it's a stomachache, I treat a stomach. If it's an eye disease, I treat eyes."

It is claimed that **Hawayo Takata** taught 12 positions (including the head, front and back of torso). Her teacher, Hayashi Chûjirô is thought to have formalised Reiki treatments in his clinic where he had two practitioner's working together on one person. His treatments are often considered to be the foundation for Reiki treatments taught in Western **branches of Reiki**.

The **ritual** of set hand placements on the body gives practitioners a structure to work from. This builds their confidence and energetic wisdom. As practitioners' inner understanding of the system of **Reiki** grows it is then possible for them to leave the ritual behind and work from a solely intuitive understanding.

Hands-on Healing

When hands are placed on or near the body during a **Reiki treatment** this is called hands-on healing. The basic premise is that **healing** exists *within* each person rather than outside. The **client**'s body draws on energy to stimulate his/her own energy via the **Reiki practitioner**'s hands. This helps move **stagnant energy** and to support balance in the body.

Hands-on healing was very popular in Japan at the turn of the 20th century. The generic Japanese word for hands-on healing is **teate**. When discussing a specifc structure to hands-on healing the word **tenohira** is used. See also **Hand Positions**.

Hanko

A hanko, displayed here, is also called an inkan and is a personal seal. This seal is used to sign formal and legal documents in conjunction with a signature. Without this seal business in Japan would stagnate. The hanko is necessary for filling in application forms or banking slips, or for when you receive registered mail. There are different kinds of hanko: cheap ready made ones – sanmon ban; ones that are officially registered – jitsu in; and those that are for banking mainly – ginkô in.

Usui Mikao would have used his hanko on his documents. The use of hanko will help modern researchers verify the authenticity of any documents that lay claim to Usui Mikao as their writer.

Hanshin Kôketsu Hô

(Japanese) Half body blood exchange **technique**.

This is a part of the technique **ketsueki kôkan hô**.

Hara

(Japanese) Belly or abdomen.

Though the abdomen is generally called the hara there are also two other energetic centers in the body. One is the head and the other is the heart.

The hara is like a battery that can be recharged through physical and spiritual **technique**s. Energy is stored at this point of the body. From here it expands throughout the entire body.

In **Usui Mikao**'s and the **Usui Reiki Ryôhô Gakkai**'s teachings many techniques are known to stimulate the hara centers. This is not unique in itself as the hara is an innate element of Japanese philosophy and culture. Whether practicing go (a Japanese game), sadô (flower arrangement), or **budô** (martial arts), the focus is on the hara.

H

Harajuku

Harajuku, Aoyama, Tôkyô. The place where **Usui Mikao** started his first official seat of learning in 1922.

Harmony

In some Japanese Reiki teachings this word is used to describe the characteristic of **SHK** and **Symbol 2**.

Harth Symbol

Non-traditional symbol used in **Karuna**

Reiki®, **Tera Mai™**, and **Karuna Ki**. It is said to help heal relationships, develop good habits, heal addictions, develop compassionate actions and to contact spiritual beings. This was the second of a number of **channel**ed **symbols** that were claimed to be retrieved by a 'Very High Being' from the Inner Planes and given to Kathleen Milner and Marcy Miller from the USA.

Hatamoto

The hatamoto were the **Shogun**'s personal guard. **Usui Mikao**'s family was hatamoto **samurai** – a high level within the ranks of samurai.

Hatsurei Hô

(Japanese) **Technique** to generate greater amounts of spiritual energy.

This technique includes the techniques **kenyoku hô**, **joshin kokyû hô** and **seishin toitsu**.

The **Usui Reiki Ryôhô Gakkai** also practice a version of this technique.

Tomita Kaiji describes another version of this technique, using **waka**, in his book *Reiki To Jinjutsu–Tomita Ryû Teate Ryôhô* that was published in 1933.

H

Hayashi Chie

The wife of **Hayashi Chûjirô**. She continued on at her husband's clinic after his death, becoming the second president of the **Hayashi Reiki Kenkyû Kai**.

Hayashi Chûjirô (1880–1940)

One of the 21 teacher students of **Usui Mikao**.

 According to **Inamoto Hyakuten** he was a **Sôtô Zen** practitioner who naturally included **Shintô** into his personal practices. According to his student, **Hawayo Takata**, Hayashi Chûjirô met and

became a student of Usui Mikao in 1925. He was a retired **naval officer** (still in the reserves) and surgeon. The length of his study with Usui Mikao was relatively short as he only studied the teachings for approximately 10 months before Usui Mikao's death in March 1926. According to **Doi Hiroshi** he was the last **Shinpiden** student of Usui Mikao. It is interesting to note that Hayashi Chûjirô didn't teach the **reiju** but instead taught an **attunement**, which included the **symbols** and **mantras** according to his students like **Yamaguchi Chiyoko**.

Once he became a **shihan** or teacher he was expected to either "engage in the spread of Reiki Ryôhô and in **Reiki treatment**s at the Gakkai Head Office" or open up his own branch. As Hayashi Chujirô was a medical **doctor** Usui Mikao felt that he should open a clinic for treatments. This, according to Doi Hiroshi, would "promote the efficacy of Reiki Ryôhô from a medical doctor's point of view". Naturally all results were to feed back to the

Usui Reiki Ryôhô Gakkai. However he broke away in 1931 developing his own branch called **Hayashi Reiki Kenkyû Kai**.

Hayashi Chûjirô was known to have created a healing guide called the *Ryôhô Shishin*. It appears to be an almost exact copy of the *Ryôhô Shishin* in the **Reiki Ryôhô Hikkei**, the healing guide from the Usui Reiki Ryôhô Gakkai. Today people believe that Hayashi Chûjirô may well have written the *Ryôhô Shishin* at Usui Mikao's request.

Hayashi Chûjirô wrote in 1938 that there were 13 fully qualified Reiki Masters but it is not known who these people were. From various reports it is believed that some of his students were **Tatsumi**, **Hawayo Takata**, **Hayashi Chie**, and **Yamaguchi Chiyoko**, and **Shûô Matsui** (not a teacher).

Hayashi Chûjirô passed away on 10 May 1940. Hawayo Takata reported that he died ceremoniously of a self-induced stroke, Yamaguchi Chiyoko recounts that he had killed himself by "breaking an artery", while others say that as he was a military man the honourable method of death would certainly have been **seppuku**.

Hayashi Reiki Kenkyû Kai

(Japanese) Hayashi Spiritual Energy Research Society.

Hayashi Chûjirô started this society in 1931 according to **Doi Hiroshi**. After his death his wife, **Hayashi Chie**, became known as the second president.

The name of his society indicates that he had adapted **Usui Mikao**'s teachings. In Japan, it is customary to keep the teaching's name intact. The name would only be changed if the teachings were similarly altered. So it is possible to see that Hayashi Chûjirô had changed the system which Usui Mikao taught. Respect, however, was definitely displayed by Hayashi Chûjirô to Usui Mikao as he always taught in front of the calligraphic scroll of Usui

Mikao's **precepts** called the **gokai no sho**.

Hayashi Chûjirô continued to use the same three **level** system as the **Usui Reiki Ryôhô Gakkai** which included **Shoden**, **Okuden** and **Shinpiden**.

H

Head Positions
See **Five Head Positions**.

Healer
Many **Reiki practitioners** struggle with the concept of whether they are healers or not. A basic principle of the system of **Reiki** is that everyone and everything is a natural healer. **Usui Mikao** is quoted in the **Reiki Ryôhô Hikkei** as saying that, "Every existence has healing power". The system of Reiki teaches how to bring awareness and strength to that quality.

Yet a practitioner never states that he/she heals someone as it is not the practitioner that is doing the healing. The practitioner facilites healing but the responsibility to heal always remains in the hands of the **client**.

Healing

The word 'heal' has many different interpretations with the word 'whole' often being used to describe it. 'To make whole' means to balance out all aspects of being human: mind, body and heart. It embraces the connectedness of each of these aspects and does not accept that one is more important than the other. The system of **Reiki** works at stimulating and strengthening each of these aspects of humanity and is therefore considered to be a system that supports and promotes healing.

One of the **five elements of Reiki** is **hands-on healing**. The other four elements of the system (**symbol**s and **mantra**s, **precepts**, **attunement**s or **reiju**, **technique**s) also support healing. Together these elements create an entire and effective system.

By focusing only on our hands within the

system of Reiki we limit our ability to heal and become whole. By strengthening and balancing our inner energy using all elements of the system of Reiki we not only affect our own lives benefically but those of everyone we come into contact with. This is healing in the microcosm (the human, the small universe) and, consequently, the macrocosm (the greater universe).

Usui Mikao is quoted as saying in the *Reiki Ryôhô Hikkei*, "Every existence has healing power. Plants, trees, animals, fish and insects but especially a human".

Healing Attunements

This non-initiatory **attunement** was developed with the intent that it focus on **healing** the self rather than the ability to 'do' **Reiki**.

However the perception that attunements give the student the ability to 'do' Reiki is not held by all systems of Reiki. There is within the system of Reiki a general understanding that everyone consists of universal energy. If this is so then all we need is **intent** when placing hands on the body to support healing by drawing on our innate ability.

Traditionally in Japan the **reiju** did not 'make' you into something eg. a **Level I** practitioner. The reiju was seen as a support for the student's personal growth.

The system of Reiki is a number of practices that when brought together teach one how to use Reiki for healing and spiritual development, this is not goverened solely by an attunement or reiju. See **Five Elements of the System of Reiki**.

Healing Crisis

See **Cleansing**.

Healing List

Non-traditional technique where a **Reiki practitioner** writes a list of people, places or things that he/she wishes to send **Reiki** to. The list is held in the hands and a **distant healing technique** is performed on it.

Healing the Past and the Future

Non-traditional technique where you send **distant healing** to yourself to heal your past, present and future.

H

Heart Sutra

A **sutra** practised in **Tendai** presenting the essence of the transcendental wisdom of the void. The Heart Surta is widely practiced in Japan and aids in the understanding of **Oneness**. The concept of Oneness lies at the base of **distant healing**.

Heaven

In Japan, Heaven is often described as one half of the universe with **Earth** being its opposite force. An ancient Japanese cosmological theory states that through the union of these dual forces all things were born.

In **Usui Mikao**'s early teachings **SHK** and **Symbol 2** are said to be associated with the energy of Heaven: intuitive and clear.

Doi Hiroshi has stated, "In the Gakkai the words 'harmony of Ten-Chi-Jin' and 'Oneness of Great Universe (the macrocosm) and Small Universe (humans or the microcosm)' are often used." Ten is Heaven, Chi is Earth, and Jin is humans.

See also **In and Yô**.

Heso Chiryô Hô

(Japanese) **Healing** at the navel **technique**.

Hibiki

(Japanese) Sound, echo, vibration.

Hibiki is sensed when the body is being scanned or treated. It may feel like heat/cold/tingling/pain/itchiness/pulsating etc... in the palm of the hand.

Hiei Zan

(Japanese) Mt Hiei near Kyôto, Japan.

There is a main **Tendai** temple complex, **enryaku ji**, on hiei zan. **Usui Mikao** is said to have studied Tendai there. It has been suggested that old **sutra** copies on hiei zan have Usui Mikao's Buddhist name on them of **Gyoho** or Gyotse.

Higher Self

Terminology used in the **New Age movement** to refer to an eternal, conscious and intelligent being. This terminology has been adopted into some recent Western **branch**es of **Reiki**.

Hikari No Kokyû Hô

(Japanese) Breathing in the light **technique**.

Also called **jôshin kokyû hô** and is a part of the technique **hatsurei hô**.

Hikkei

(Japanese) Companion, often called manual in the West.

See *Reiki Ryôhô Hikkei*.

Hiragana

Hiragana is used to write the inflectional endings of the conceptual words that are written in **kanji**. It is also used for all types of native words not written in kanji. This was an attempt to cut down on the amount of kanji needed to express a multisyllabic Japanese word.

Ho

(Japanese) Symbol.

This word is used to refer to the **symbol**s taught in the system of **Reiki** in **Gendai Reiki Hô**.

Hô

(Japanese) Method or **technique**.

This word is used in the description of a number of Japanese Reiki techniques.

Hokke-Zanmai

(Japanese) The lotus samadhi.

A **meditation technique** based on the Lotus **Sutra**. One chants the Lotus Sutra while circumambulating the temple hall. This meditation is said to have been practiced by **Usui Mikao**. **Zazen Shikan Taza** is a modern simplified form of the Hokke-Zanmai which excludes a lot of the more difficult elements of the practice (for a complete version of the Zazen Shikan Taza see *The Reiki Sourcebook*)

Hotsuma Tsutae

Its first parts, *Book of Heaven* and *Book of Earth*, were recorded and edited around 660 BC (according to the Nihonshoki calendar) by Kushimikatama-Wanihiko. His descendant, Ootataneko, recorded the third part, *Book of Man*, which contains the stories after Emperor Jinmu (660 BC), and offered the complete *Hotsuma Tsutae* to Emperor Keiko (the twelfth emperor) in AD 126. The origin of the *Hotsuma Tsutae* is controversial. It is guessed to be very old while some researchers challenge the dates written above. Copies of *Hotsuma Tsutae* have been stored in iwamuro (cave storage) in a Tendai temple at **enryaku ji** (**hiei zan**, Kyôto). These copies may have been given to Saichô (767–822), the founding priest of enryaku ji. Tendai priests were also known to give lectures on the *Hotsuma Tsutae*.

Hrih

(Sanskrit) This is an ancient Indian seed

syllable (a syllable used for **meditation**).

The Japanese seed syllable **kiriku** is derived from the hrih. **Symbol 2** appears to have evolved from the kiriku.

HSZSN

As the **mantra**s of the system of **Reiki** are commonly classified as **sacred**, pseudonyms are used in the *A-Z of Reiki* rather than the true mantras. The pseudonym for the third **traditional** mantra is the initials HSZSN.

The kanji of the true mantra of HSZSN is actually **Symbol 3**.

The main Western characteristic of HSZSN is as the Distance Symbol and it is spoken three times in conjunction with Symbol 3.

The main Japanese characteristic is **Connection**. In Japan, the mantra is not necessarily used in conjunction with the symbol. The early teachings of **Usui Mikao** claim that HSZSN develops a **Reiki practitioner**'s link to the energy of the **Heart**.

It is within our heart that we embrace the concept of **Oneness.**

This mantra and its kanji are used in many aspects of the Japanese culture, one of them being Ninjutsu. This kanji can also be found in Stephen Turnbull's book *The True Story of Japan's Secret Warrior Cult* on Ninjutsu.

Hui Yin Breath

Non-traditional breath **technique** introduced via the **New Age movement** into the **attunement** process of some modern **branches of Reiki** including **Raku Kei Reiki**. This technique originally comes from China and lies at the base of practices such as Chinese **Qi Gong**. It stimulates the energy to rise up the back energy channel and harmonise with the energy descending down the front energy channel, helping to balance the body's energy.

I

Iava Symbol

Non-traditional symbol used in **Karuna Reiki®**, **Tera Mai™**, and **Karuna Ki**. It is claimed to heal co-dependence, empower goals and heal the **Earth**. Catherine Mills Bellamont from Ireland **channel**ed this **symbol**.

Ichinyo

(Japanese) **Oneness**.

The concept of Oneness is linked to the **HSZSN** and **Symbol 3** in **Usui Mikao**'s early teachings. When working with this concept we start to realise the non-existence of 'I'. When the 'I' disappears the notion of 'others' will disappear too. Once this occurs it is no longer possible to make the separation between 'I' and 'others', and there arises the desire to protect and help others as oneself.

Imperial Rescript on Education

The Imperial Rescript was written by the **Meiji Emperor** in 1890 and is an edict that became a fundamental Japanese moral code until the end of World War II.

Kanô Jigorô, the founder of **jûdô**, also used this text as a moral code in his teachings. There are claims that he was an acquaintance of **Usui Mikao**.

According to one **Reiki** researcher the **five precepts** are based on this rescript.

In

(Japanese) A physical sign often using the hands.

More commonly known in the West by its **Sanskrit** name of **mudra**.

Inamoto, Reverend Hyakuten

Teacher of **Komyo Reiki Kai**. He has studied the system of **Reiki** under **Yamaguchi Chiyoko**. He is also a translator for **Doi Hiroshi** and a **Pure Land Buddhist** monk.

Hyakuten Inamoto's translation of the **memorial stone** and the **Meiji Emperor**'s **waka** is included in *The Reiki Sourcebook*.

In and Yô

(Japanese) Yin and yang.

These are the cosmic dual forces of **Heaven** and **Earth**. The **samurai** of the 17th century used these principles along with Chinese Confucianism. The first two **mantras** and **symbols** in Usui Mikao's early teachings are said to help the student become One with in and yô.

Doi Hiroshi wrote in his book *Iyashino Gendai Reiki-ho* that, "Usui-sensei gave his training based on the truth that heaven and earth's nature makes humans greater."

It is believed that Usui Mikao deliberately created a system that was unaligned to any specific religion. However, he naturally drew elements from his personal religious and energetic experiences to create the system. To develop a practice in this way was quite common in Japan. Some of his influences were **Buddhism**, **Shintô**, martial arts and **Shugendô**. The book *Religions of Japan in Practice* states, "Japanese religious practice drew from many sources, accommodating both the imported religion of Buddhism and the native Shintô tradition, while accepting Chinese yin-yang beliefs and other aspects of religious Taoism."

Independent Reiki Master

Independent Reiki Master is a term used to

describe people who are **Reiki Masters** but are not aligned with a particular **branch of Reiki**. They might use an eclectic approach drawing on **technique**s from many branches and/or include **New Age movement** practices. The vast majority of Reiki Masters in the West are Independent Reiki Masters.

Individual Attunement

An **attunement** is a **ritual** performed on students (often on their back and front while they are seated) by **Reiki Masters**. This ritual is generally performed as an individual attunement meaning that the teacher completes the attunement on each student individually before moving to the next student. With the advent of large class sizes some teachers began to line students up and walk down the front of the line – performing the first part of the attunement and then walking down the back of the line – completing the back.

Some teachers have expressed concern that

the individual energetic link between teacher and student is broken or weakened by this 'group' method.

Initiation

This word is often used to describe the Japanese **reiju** and/ or the Western **attunement** process. Its Latin origins mean 'beginning'.

Integrated Attunement

Attunement created and taught by **Doi Hiroshi** in the **gokui kaiden** level of **Gendai Reiki Hô**. It integrates all **mantra**s and **symbol**s into one attunement.

Intent

A **Reiki practitioner** sets intent by anticipating an outcome. This anticipation guides the practitioner in his/her planned course of action.

The clearer a practitioner's energy becomes through self-practice, the more focused, and therefore more effective, the intent is.

T'ai Chi Classics describes intention thus, "The intention directs the chi, the chi directs the body".

Ishikuro, Iris (?-1984)

One of **Hawayo Takata**'s 22 **Reiki Master** students. She was the tenth Master to be trained by Hawayo Takata. She was told to only train three people to the Master level. Iris Ishikuro trained just two people to this level, her daughter and **Arthur Robertson**.

Arthur Robertson worked with Iris Ishikuro and together they had an immense impact on the future of the system of **Reiki** with their system **Raku Kei Reiki**. They introduced a great deal of what is called 'Tibetan' information into the system. This included the 'Tibetan' **symbol**s, the **Johre symbol** and 'Tibetan' techniques such as **breath of the fire dragon** and the **hui yin breath**. Iris Ishikuro died in 1984.

Islam

The system of **Reiki** is not a religion and is used by people of all religions around the world.

Ittôen

Eguchi Toshihiro, a friend and student of **Usui Mikao**, taught a form of **hands-on healing** to the Ittôen community. Some families still practice this today although there are only about 100 residents remaining in the community. The present leader is the grandson of the founder, Nishida Tenko, and his name is Takeshi. This is a photo of Nishida Tenko.

According to **Professor J. Rabinovitch** the Ittôen community is not a religion but more of a philosophical system. At its core are popular **Buddhism**, Zen Buddhism, Confuscianism, and even some Christian teachings.

J

Jakikiri Jôka Hô

(Japanese) A **technique** that energetically cleanses and enhances inanimate objects.

Jikiden Reiki

Jikiden Reiki means '**Reiki** as taught or initiated' by **Hayashi Chûjirô**. **Yamaguchi Tadao** is teaching this in Japan and the West today. He was taught Reiki by his mother, **Yamaguchi Chiyoko**.

Both Yamaguchi Chiyoko and her uncle, Sugano Wasaburo, studied with Hayashi Chûjirô. Only Sugano Wasaburo officially reached the teacher level. Yamaguchi Chiyoko was taught how to perform the **attunement** by him.

Jiko Joka Hô

(Japanese) Self-purification **technique**.

Jiro Asuke

A well-known **hands-on healing** student of **Tomita Kaiji**. Tomita Kaiji was a student of **Usui Mikao**.

Jisshû Kai

(Japanese) Practice or training meetings.

The **Usui Reiki Ryôhô Gakkai** once held jisshû kai. These practice meetings, where **technique**s were taught and practiced, took place after the **shûyô kai** or the group meetings.

Jôdo Shû

(Japanese) School of the **Pure Land sect**.

Johrei Reiki

Johrei Reiki was developed from **Raku Kei Reiki** using what is called the **Johre**

(Johrei) **symbol** as part of its practices and **attunement**s.

The inspiration for this **Reiki** system was the Johrei fellowship, a spiritual **healing** practice developed in 1935 in Japan by Mokichi Okada. It also uses a form of **reiju**.

Once the Johrei fellowship discovered this unauthorized use of their name the system changed its name to **Vajra Reiki**.

Johre Symbol

Non-traditional symbol said to have been added by **Arthur Robertson** who created **Raku Kei Reiki** with **Iris Ishikuro**. It is said to release **blockage**s.

This **symbol** has been taken from the Johrei fellowship and is also known as the White Light Symbol. It was taught in **Johrei Reiki**.

Jôshin Kokyû Hô

(Japanese) **Technique** to **focus** the mind with the breath.

Also called **hikari no kokyû hô** and is a part of **hatsurei hô**.

Judaism

The system of **Reiki** is not a religion and is used by people of all religions around the world. There is even a **branch of Reiki** based on the Hebrew alphabet called **Alef Reiki**.

Jûdô

Modernized, sport oriented form of jujutsu. Founded by **Kanô Jigorô** who is said to have been an acquaintance of **Usui Mikao**.

Jumon

(Japanese) Spell, incantation.

Jumon is a sound that invokes a specific energetic vibration. In Western forms of the system of **Reiki** it is commonly called by the **Sanskrit** word **mantra**.

In **Usui Mikao**'s early teachings it is said that the jumon made the teachings more accessible for **Shintô** followers. They can be used as a focus point for **meditation**.

According to **Suzuki san** it was **Eguchi Toshihiro** who introduced the three **Okuden** jumon to Usui Mikao.

J

Kaicho

(Japanese) Title of the president of the **Usui Reiki Ryôhô Gakkai**.

Kaimyô

(Japanese) A posthumous Buddhist name.

Also called Hômyô. It is a posthumous Buddhist name given to the soul of the newly departed person by the priest at a funeral.

Originally it was a Buddhist name given to devout believers who took the Buddhist **precepts**.

Each **sect** has its own way of giving kaimyô, but as a rule it is made up of several **kanji**.

Usui Mikao's kaimyo is **Reizan-in Shuyo Tenshin Koji**.

Kaisho

(Japanese) **Kanji** in modern, standard style.

This style is similar to the printed style of kanji, and is taught in schools.

Kanji

(Japanese) Kanji are Japanese written characters that are both pictographs (pictures that represent ideas) and ideographs (symbols that represent the sounds that form its name).

K

In China, kanji originated in the Yellow River area about 2000 BC. During the third and fourth centuries AD it was brought across from China and Korea to Japan. Until this time Japan had only ever used the spoken language. The Chinese characters were used phonetically to represent similar sounding Japanese syllables, the actual meaning of the characters were ignored.

Kanji Hand Mudras

Kanji are Japanese written characters. **Mudra**

is a **Sanskrit** word and represents the stimulating of specific energy through body postures and hand movements.

Kanji Hand Mudras were introduced to the system of **Reiki** in an Omega Dawn Sanctuary of Healing Arts manual in 1983 from the branch **Raku Kei Reiki** according to **Robert Fueston**. This manual was created by **Arthur Robertson** in conjunction with **Iris Ishikuro**.

Kannon

This **deity** is sometimes taught as the connection to **Symbol 3**. Kannon is the 'Bodhisattva who Perceives the Sounds of the World'.

Kanô Jigorô (1860–1938)

The founder of **jûdô**. There are some claims that he knew **Usui Mikao**. It was once thought that Kanô Jigorô was in a photo with Usui Mikao from **Mochizuki Toshitaka**'s book *Chô Kantan Iyashi No Te*. This however could not be verified by the Kodokan Jûdô Institute in Japan.

Karuna Ki

A recently developed **non-traditional** practice inspired by the system of **Reiki** and influenced by **Karuna Reiki®**. It is known as The Way of Compassionate Energy. Some of the non-traditional **symbols** taught at this **level** are **Halu, Iava, Rama, Sati, Shanti**, and **Zonar**.

Karuna Reiki®

A **non-traditional** practice inspired by the system of **Reiki** that utilizes a number of non-traditional Reiki **symbols**. Some of the non-traditional symbols taught at this level are **Halu, Iava, Rama, Sati, Shanti**, and **Zonar**. Some of the non-traditional practices taught are **toning** and the **violet breath**. Karuna Reiki® is the registered trademark of the International Center for Reiki Training.

Its influences are from both **Tera Mai™ Reiki** and **Usui Shiki Ryôhô**.

K

Katakana

Katakana became phonetic shorthand based on Chinese characters (**kanji**). It was used by students who, while listening to classic Buddhist lectures, would make notations on the pronunciations or meanings of unfamiliar characters, and sometimes wrote commentaries between the lines of certain passages.

Katsu

This is a method of infusing life into a person and is mentioned on page 35 of **Hayashi Chûjirô's** *Ryôhô Shishin* as a method to aid resuscitation.

Kenkyû Kai

(Japanese) Research or study society.

This is the name that the **Usui Reiki Ryôhô Gakkai** uses today for its regular meetings. Previously these meetings were called **shuyô kai**.

Kenyoku Hô

(Japanese) Dry bathing or brushing off **technique**.

This is similar to purification methods practiced in **Shintô**. Purification rites are a vital part of Shintô. A personal purification rite might be purification by water also known as **misogi**. This would involve standing under a waterfall.

K

Ketsueki Kôkan Hô

(Japanese) Blood exchange **technique**.

Variations are **hanshin kôketsu hô**, **zenshin kôketsu hô**, **finishing treatment** or **nerve stroke**. Also called **kôketsu hô**.

Ki

(Japanese) Universal energy.

In Japan, ki is considered to be an integral element in the success of daily life. Many Japanese traditions are based on a strong connection to ki. Apart from martial arts and religious training, the success of the Japanese tea ceremony, the ancient game of go and the art of calligraphy are all based on the practitioner's ability to **channel** free-flowing ki.

Ki Ko

(Japanese) **Qi Gong** or energy cultivation.

These **technique**s have their origins in Chinese physical and meditative practices called Qi Gong. They help to regulate the body, mind and breath and are both Taoist and Buddhist in origin.

Kiriku

A seed syllable is a letterform used solely for **meditation** and is a part of esoteric **Buddhism** practiced in China and Japan. It is the topmost image in the photo. Its **Sanskrit** origins can be traced back to the seed syllable **hrih**.

The kiriku calls upon the energy of **Amida Nyorai**. Amida Nyorai is the main deity in **Pure Land** Buddhism.

Symbol 2 in the system of **Reiki** appears to be derived from the kiriku.

Koizumi Tetsutarô

Mochizuki Toshitaka has listed a number of early Japanese **Reiki practitioner**s in his book *Chô Kantan Iyashi No Te*. He relates that Koizumi Tetsutarô was a member of the **Usui Reiki Ryôhô Gakkai** and taught **Reiki** at their headquarters and in regional areas.

Kôketsu Hô

(Japanese) An abbreviation of **ketsueki kôkan hô**.

Kôki

(Japanese) Second half.

The second part or grade within **Okuden**.

Koki Hô

(Japanese) Sending **ki** with the breath **technique**.

Komyo Reiki Kai

A Japanese **branch of Reiki** developed by **Inamoto Hyakuten** from **Yamaguchi Chiyoko**'s teachings. The motto of this branch is "Go placidly in the midst of praise or blame" which Inamoto Hyakuten explains is a form of **anshin ritsumei**.

Kondô Masaki

Seventh and current president of the **Usui Reiki Ryôhô Gakkai**. He is also a University Professor.

Koriki Symbol

Non-traditional symbol taught in **Reido Reiki**. Also called 'the force of happiness'.

Kotodama

(Japanese) Words carrying spirit.

Doi Hiroshi uses the word kotodama rather than jumon to address the **mantra**s taught in the system of **Reiki**. **Ueshiba Morihei**, the founder of **aikidô** who is said to have been an acquaintance of **Usui Mikao**, also used kotodama in his teachings. He belonged to the **Oomoto sect** who had formulated effective **meditation technique**s and powerful chants based on kotodama. Kotodama in **Shintô** invoke specific energies/deities.

Koyama Kimiko (1906–99).

Sixth president of the **Usui Reiki Ryôhô Gakkai**. According to her student, **Doi Hiroshi**, she always said that "Reiki is the light of love".

In **Mochizuki Toshitaka**'s book *Chô Kantan Iyashi No Te* he states that as president she held meetings four times a month.

For the 50th anniversary of the Usui Reiki Ryôhô Gakkai, Koyama Kimiko published the

Reiki Ryôhô Hikkei for members. The *shiori* booklet, created for society members, was also written by Koyama Kimiko and **Wanami Hôichi**.

Kriya Symbol

Non-traditional symbol used in **Karuna Reiki®**, **Tera Mai™**, and **Karuna Ki**. It is said to ground, manifest goals, create priorities and heal the human race.

Kuboi, Harry M.

The sixth of **Hawayo Takata's** 22 **Reiki Master** students. He was trained to the Master **level** in April 1977.

Harry Kuboi believes that 99 per cent of people who learn the system of **Reiki** have 'negative' Reiki and therefore doesn't teach it anymore. Instead he does exorcisms where people's 'negative' Reiki becomes 'positive'.

He told **Robert Fueston** that **Barbara Weber Ray** had sent him a letter stating that if he wanted to become a certified Reiki Master he would have to re-train with her and pay several thousand dollars.

He also said that he had **channel**ed **Usui Mikao** who gave him the title of 'Reiki Master of Masters'.

K

Robert Fueston was further told that he could be trained to the Master Level for US$10,000 but he would have to receive a Reiki exorcism first. He would not be allowed to train others as a Reiki Master after this either.

Kun Yomi

Here Chinese **kanji** are used to express Japanese words that have a similar meaning to the original Chinese word. When a Japanese word's sound uses kanji this is then called a kun yomi reading.

Kurama Yama

(Japanese) Mt Kurama near Kyôto, Japan.

It states on the **memorial stone** of **Usui Mikao** that he became enlightened while performing a **meditation** on kurama yama. According to the Kurama Temple (in the photo), Usui Mikao has no specific connection to them.

Many martial arts practitioners, like Ueshiba Morihei, also practiced on kurama yama.

Kushu Shinren

(Japanese) Painful and difficult training.

A form of **shûgyô**. Kushu shinren was the word used on the **memorial stone** for **Usui Mikao**'s practice on **kurama yama**.

L

Leiki

Hawayo Takata sometimes wrote Leiki instead of **Reiki**. This seems to be a translation mistake. To pronounce the word, Reiki, in Japanese it is necessary to forego any preconceptions about language that you may have. The first sound in 'rei' is neither an 'R' nor an 'L', as some Westerners believe. In Japanese the sound is in fact somewhere in between the two letters. The Japanese language has no correlation with English or its pronunciations. The kanji for 'rei' is officially spelt with an 'R' when translating into English and is therefore pronounced with an 'R' (even though the Japanese pronunciation might sound similar to what is understood as an 'L' in English).

Level

There are three levels of training with the system of **Reiki** with some branches dividing these levels up.

Between each level students are required to practice the **technique**s and principles that they have been taught as preparation for moving forward to the next level.

In the West the levels have varying names including degree or facet. In Japan, the three major levels are called **Shoden**, **Okuden** and **Shinpiden**.

In the **Usui Reiki Ryôhô Gakkai** manual, called the *Reiki Ryôhô Hikkei*, **Usui Mikao** is quoted as saying, "I will teach it (**Okuden**, **Level II**) to people who have learned **Shoden** (**Level I**) and who are good students, good conduct and enthusiasts."

Level I

Called **Shoden** in some Japanese branches. Students are taught how to heal themselves and friends and family. They are given a **self-healing** practice routine to continue and develop before moving on to **Level II**.

Level II

Called **Okuden** in some Japanese branches. Students are taught the three **mantra**s and **symbol**s and how to put these to practice. Once again students are asked to develop their personal practice before moving to **Level III**.

Level III

Called **Shinpiden** in some Japanese branches. Here students are taught the fourth **mantra** and **symbol** and how to perform **attunement**s or **reiju** and teach.

Lineage

Teachings that are handed down to a student are the student's 'lineage'. A lineage is expressed as a list of teacher's names in chronological order. The lineage should be able to be traced back to the founder of the system, in the case of the system of **Reiki** this is **Usui Mikao**.

In the West an imbalance has developed in the teachings. The importance of the **attunement** has grown disproportionately to the rest of the Reiki teachings. In fact many people today say "I've had my **Level I** attunement therefore I am now a **Reiki practitioner**". What has actually occurred is that they have completed a course (which included attunements) and they have now set off on the path of a Reiki practitioner. In this case some of the modern Western Reiki teachings believe that an attunement 'makes' you into something eg. a Level I or II practitioner. Here the idea of the attunement being the course itself has taken over.

In the earlier teachings of **Usui Mikao** an attunement or **reiju** is performed to support a practitioner in his/her practice. For this reason the **Usui Reiki Ryôhô Gakkai** (that still exists today) offers **reiju** to members at each gathering.

Therefore the lineage of a student will depend upon the teachings that the student has received. This means not just the style of attunement or reiju, or just the **five elements of the system of Reiki** or even just the energy of the teacher. It is the entire teachings that are being handed down. This is what a student has acquired by the time he or she walks out of the door.

L

Ling Chi

(Chinese) This is the pronunciation of the two **kanji** that represent the word '**Reiki**' in Chinese.

Ling Chi is also used in a similar context. Daniel Reed states in his book *Chi-Gung: Harnessing the Power of the Universe* that, "Ling-chi is the subtlest and most highly refined of all the energies in the human system and the product of the most advanced stages of practice, whereby the ordinary energies of the body are transformed into pure spiritual vitality."

Lombardi, Ethel

She was the second of **Hawayo Takata**'s 22 **Reiki Master** students. In 1976 she became a Reiki Master and went on to create a system called MariEL. Though this was based on the system of **Reiki** it was filled out with her own interpretations. She did not wish to be a member of any of the post-Hawayo Takata organizations.

Lotus Sutra

A **sutra** practiced in **Tendai**. In Japanese it is called the Hoke-kyo or Myohorenge kyo and forms the basis on which Tendai is established.

Love and Light

The salutation 'Love and Light' is used by some **Reiki practitioner**s in the West.

Curiously this salutation has similarities to

the characteristics of the deities who represent **kurama yama**. These three characteristics are power, light and love. Kurama yama is where the **memorial stone** states that **Usui Mikao** meditated.

L

M

Making Contact with Higher Beings

Non-traditional technique of connecting and asking for guidance from higher beings.

Manifesting

Non-traditional technique to manifest what you need or want.

Mantra

It is a power-laden syllable or series of syllables that manifest certain cosmic forces. Traditionally, there are only four **mantras** in Usui Mikao's teachings. The mantras were given to students as a device for tapping into specific elements of energy.

In some Japanese **branches of Reiki** the mantras are practiced independently of the

symbols. However, in the West, the mantra is chanted three times as the symbol is drawn.

The Japanese words to describe the word mantra are either **kotodama** or **jumon**.

Master Symbol

This name is sometimes applied to **DKM** and **Symbol 4** in Western forms of the system of **Reiki**.

In Japan its characteristic is considered to be **Empowerment**.

M

Matsui Shûô

He studied with **Hayashi Chûjirô** in 1928. His first **level** was completed in five lots of one and a half hour sessions. Matsui Shûô wrote in an article called *Treatment to Heal Diseases, Hand Healing* in the magazine *Sunday Mainichi*, 4 March 1928 about the levels **Shoden** and **Okuden**.

McCullough, Barbara Lincoln

One of **Hawayo Takata**'s 22 **Reiki Master** students.

McFadyen, Mary Alexandra

One of **Hawayo Takata**'s 22 **Reiki Master** students. She took her second level training with **John Harvey Gray** and her Master Level with **Hawayo Takata**. According to **Robert Fueston**, Mary McFadyen has written two German Reiki books entitled *Die Heilkraft des Reiki. Lehren einer Meisterin* and *Die Heilkraft des Reiki. Mit Händen heilen. Schnellbehandlung.*

Meditation

Some practices taught in the system of **Reiki** are meditation practices. Depending on the **branch of Reiki** their origins may be Japanese or taken from other cultural and spiritual backgrounds.

Meiji

(Japanese) Name of an era.

Meiji Emperor (1852–1912)

The Meiji Emperor ruled Japan from 1867–1912. **Usui Mikao**, **Eguchi Toshihiro** (Usui Mikao's friend and student), **Tomita Kaiji** and the **Usui Reiki Ryôhô Gakkai** used **waka** written by the Meiji Emperor in their teachings. This poetry was called **gyosei**.

M

Memorial Stone

This is the engraved memorial stone relating elements of **Usui Mikao**'s life from a gravesite at the **Pure Land** Buddhist **Saihôji Temple** in Tôkyô. The top section of the memorial stone can be seen in the photo.

The stone was placed there by a number of Usui Mikao's students just one year after his death in 1927. The memorial stone is one aspect of Usui Mikao's life as seen through the eyes of his students from the **Usui Reiki Ryôhô Gakkai**. Some state that the students who wrote this information did not consult with Usui Mikao's family and therefore may have left out information that was relevant in a memorial about his life.

Menkyo Kaiden

(Japanese) Licence of complete and total transmission.

It is a **certificate** given in traditional arts to show full proficiency for a **lineage** or style. It normally denotes a licence indicating a very high level of skill. For some lineages, it might be given to the headmaster. It is said that **Usui**

Mikao received menkyo kaiden in a specific branch of martial arts.

Mental/Emotional Symbol

The name is sometimes applied to **SHK** and **Symbol 2** in Western forms of the system of **Reiki**.

In Japan its characteristic is considered to be **Harmony**.

Meridians

M

These are interconnected energy lines in the body. This understanding of the body's energetic system originates from traditional Chinese medicine.

Metta Meditation

Non-traditional meditation focusing on good-will and sending love and compassion to all beings.

Mikkyô

(Japanese) The secret teaching, esoteric **Buddhism**.

There are five general areas taught in **Tendai**. They are the teachings of the **Lotus Sutra**; esoteric Mikkyô practices; **meditation** practices; **precepts**; and **Pure Land** teachings.

This form of Buddhism reached Japan at the beginning of the ninth century. There is a clear connection between **Usui Mikao**'s teachings and Mikkyô. For example: the physical aspects of the **reiju** called **go shimbô** and the origins of the fourth **jumon DKM**.

If, as is claimed, Usui Mikao was a Tendai lay priest he would have studied Mikkyô as it is an integral part of Tendai.

Mine Imae

According to **Mochizuki Toshitaka**'s book, *Chô Kantan Iyashi No Te* she was a musician and the wife of fellow **Reiki practitioner Mine Umataro**. In 1967 specific details about **Usui**

Mikao's students were written of in her book *Kyujyu Nen No Ayumi*. She was involved with teaching Reiki until the age of 103.

Mine Umataro (1865-1934)

According to **Mochizuki Toshitaka**'s book, *Chô Kantan Iyashi No Te*, he was one of the teachers of the **Usui Reiki Ryôhô Gakkai**. Mochizuki Toshitaka's book also includes a full page photo of him. His wife, **Mine Imae**, also taught **Reiki**.

M

Misogi

(Japanese) Purification.

Purification rites are a vital part of **Shintô**. A personal purification rite is purification by water; this may involve standing under a waterfall, which is known as **misogi**.

In **Usui Mikao**'s teachings there is a **technique** called **kenyoku hô** – a method of dry bathing or brushing off, which is a form of misogi. Shintô priests practice techniques such as kenyoku hô.

One Shintô practitioner said that he performed a similar ritual with a group of men from his village where they wore only a red loincloth at the hekogaki festival (putting on the loincloth festival).

Mitchell, Paul

One of **Hawayo Takata**'s 22 **Reiki Master** students. He studied **Level I** in 1978 and later became a Reiki Master in November of 1979 in San Francisco, California. He is a founding member of **The Reiki Alliance** and works closely with **Phyllis Lei Furumoto**.

Robert Fueston states that Paul Mitchell and **George Araki** received their Reiki Master **attunement** together in November 1979 at Paul Mitchell's house in San Fransisco while **Fran Brown** waited in another room.

Mitsui Kôshi

A student of **Eguchi Toshihiro**. According to a

recently published Japanese book by Mihashi Kazuo on the life of Eguchi Toshihiro, Mitsui Kôshi was a village mayor who wrote and reviewed **waka**. He introduced Eguchi Toshihiro's teachings in a book which increased their popularity and he also helped facilitate the actual teachings.

He was also a good friend of fellow student **Miyazaki Gorô**.

Mitsui Mieko

A Japanese **Reiki practitioner** living in New York, who visited her native country in 1985. She began a revival of the system of **Reiki** in Japan by teaching the first two two **level**s of **The Radiance Technique**.

Here, she met **Ogawa Fumio**, a member of the **Usui Reiki Ryôhô Gakkai**. In 1986 there was an article in a Japanese magazine called *Twilight Zone* with a photo of her practicing the system of Reiki and of Ogawa Fumio reading a book written by the founder of The Radiance

Technique. **Doi Hiroshi** claims to have been one of the first Japanese to study **Level**s I and II with Mieko Mitsui.

Miyazaki Gorô

Student of **Eguchi Toshihiro**. According to a recently published Japanese book by Mihashi Kazuo on the life of Eguchi Toshihiro, Miyazaki Gorô was married to the daughter of Eguchi Toshihiro. He also wrote **waka** and books, and got on very well with a fellow student called **Mitsui Kôshi**.

After Eguchi Toshihiro's death he focused more on writing than the actual teaching of the practices.

The popularity of Eguchi Toshihiro's teachings gradually tapered away after Miyazake Gorô's death.

Mochizuki Toshitaka

Writer of two Japanese Reiki books and founder of the Vortex school in Japan. In his

2001 book, *Chô Kantan Iyashi No Te*, there is a photo of **Usui Mikao** and 19 of his students, family and friends in 1926. In the first edition of this book **Iyashi No Te (Healing Hands)**, Mochizuki Toshitaka claims to have healed 3000 people. In his 2001 condensed version with pictures he claims to have healed up to 5200 people.

Reiki To Jinjutsu–Tomita Ryû Teate Ryôhô (*Reiki and Humanitarian Work–Tomita Ryû Hands Healing*), a book written by **Tomita Kaiji** in 1933 was re-published in 1999 with the help of Mochizuki Toshitaka. Included in this book are many anecdotes about **healing**, **hand positions** for specific diseases and an interesting version of the **technique hatsurei hô**.

Mon or Kamon

(Japanese) Family crest.

Mon originated in the 11th century when court nobles and warriors used emblems as **symbols** of their families. The designs were drawn from a variety of objects like the sun, moon, stars, animals, geometrical patterns and letters. Families marked their clothing, banners and many other things with their crest.

The most famous crest is the 16-petalled chrysanthemum possessed by the Imperial family.

Usui Mikao's **Chiba** crest is a circle with a dot at the top. The circle represents the universe, and the dot or Japanese star represents the North Star. The North Star never moves while the universe circumambulates it.

Money and Reiki

It is believed that **Usui Mikao** initially saw his teachings as spiritual practices which he himself undertook and also passed onto others. There was no formalized system at this point.

Once he began teaching the Japanese **naval officers** this changed. At least one healing guide was written up and a formal **dôjô** was created. There are no records available that state if he did or didn't charge for his teachings and **healings**. From a sensible perspective money would have had to come from somewhere to maintain the dôjô whether that was from patrons, students or **clients**.

After Usui Mikao died the **Usui Reiki Ryôhô Gakkai** is known to have charged large sums of money for the teachings. There is an account from an article written in 1928 where a famous Japanese playwright studied with the society (with **Hayashi Chûjirô** in fact) and questioned why it was so expensive. **Professsor J. Rabinovitch** states that in **Eguchi Toshihiro**'s diaires she learnt that he actually resigned from the society because he could not understand why a well-to-do naval officer would charge so much money. As Eguchi Toshihiro was a friend of Usui Mikao's, his resignation from the society would signify that Usui Mikao had not charged his students and clients large sums of money.

Hawayo Takata had more or less regular

fees that she charged her students. She supposedly requested that her students ask the same fees she had.

There has always been controversy over the pricing of **Reiki courses** and **Reiki treatments**. Today some feel that they should all be free and others believe that $10,000, Hawayo Takata's asking price, should be required for a **Reiki Master** class.

You cannot pay for energy – it is subjective and intangible. For this reason a sensible suggestion is that the **client** and student pay only for the *quality* of the treatment or course that they receive.

Morning Prayer

Non-traditional prayer to be practiced each morning. This is a prayer that is practiced in **Satya Reiki**.

Mudra

(Sanskrit) **Ritual**istic signs performed with the

fingers and hands.

Some **branches of Reiki** have added mudras into their practice and teachings. However in traditional Eastern practices like esoteric **Buddhism**, martial arts or **Qi Gong**, these mudras are only taught to students who have a deep understanding of emptiness or void. If the student has not integrated emptiness into the mind, body, or spirit, then practising a mudra is useless.

M

Muryo-Ju

(Japanese) Infinite life and light.

This is another name for **Amida Buddha**. It is also the name (not **mantra**) of **Symbol 2** taught in **Komyo Reiki Kai**.

N

Nadete Chiryô Hô
(Japanese) Stroking with the hands **technique**.

Nagana Harue
Student of **Usui Mikao** according to **Doi Hiroshi**.

Nagao Tatseyi
He completed **Levels I** and **II** with **Hawayo Takata** in Hawaii and while in Japan in 1950 received **Shinpiden** (Master or teacher level) from **Hayashi Chie** (**Hayashi Chûjirô**'s wife). He returned to Hawaii to teach the system of **Reiki** to students and died in 1980. This is stated by William Lee Rand.

Nakano
A suburb of Tôkyô where **Usui Mikao** moved

his **dôjô** to in February 1925 according to the **memorial stone**.

Naval Officers

In 1922, **Usui Mikao** formalized his teachings and began to teach **hands-on healing** to a group of naval officers. These men went on to create the **Usui Reiki Ryôhô Gakkai** claiming Usui Mikao as their first president. The society still exists in Japan today.

A member of the original society was **Hayashi Chûjirô** whose teachings created the backbone for Western forms of Reiki. **Inamoto Hyakuten** believes that what is taught as Usui's Reiki in the West could actually be called Hayashi's Reiki.

Nentatsu Hô

(Japanese) A **technique** to send thoughts.

Also called **seiheki chiryô hô**.

Nerve Stroke

Also called **finishing stroke**, zenshin kôketsu
hô or **ketsueki kôkan hô**. **Hawayo Takata**
taught this **technique** in **Level II**.

New Age Movement

The search for universal truths in the 20th
century created a loose network of spiritual
teachers, **healer**s and searchers. They have
become known as the New Age movement
and draw on mythical and religious historical
material to develop their understandings of life.
From 1980 onward the New Age Movement
has had a great impact on the system of **Reiki**.

New Religions

In Japan, the term 'new religions' relates to all
sects founded since the middle of the 19th
century. In Japanese they are called shinshûkyô.
It includes a great diversity of sects. Most are
influenced by much older traditional religions
including **Shintô**, **Buddhism** and **Shugendô**.

Some well known new religions are **Oomoto**, Shunmei, Tenrikyo and Mahikari.

The system of **Reiki**, though not a religion, has some similarities to these new religions as it, too, has drawn on traditional Japanese religious elements. Some similar elements include the system's practice of **hands-on healing**, **jumon** and **kotodama** use, and even the **reiju**.

Non-traditional

This term is used in the *A-Z of Reiki* to represent teachings that are not directly related to the Japanese origins of the system of **Reiki**. The term largely includes add-ons from the **New Age movement**.

O

Ogawa Fumio (1908-1998)

Member of the **Usui Reiki Ryôhô Gakkai** who by 1943 completed six grades of proficiency (two **levels**) in 14 months. His **certificates** were displayed in a Japanese magazine called *Twilight Zone* in 1986. In the same magazine was a photo of him reading a book written by the founder of a Western style of Reiki called **The Radiance Technique**. Ogawa Fumio's stepfather, **Ogawa Kôzô**, ran a **healing** center in Shizuoka during **Usui Mikao**'s lifetime.

Ogawa Fumio's certificates read rokkyû, gokyû, yonkyû, sankyû, **Okuden zenki** and Okuden **kôki**. The first four were grades within the **Level I**. The last two were grades within the **Level II**. These dated from 1942 to 1943.

Accoding to **Mochizuki Toshitaka**, in

1991 he self-published a book called *Reiki Wa Darenidemo Deru.*

Ogawa Kôzô

The stepfather of **Ogawa Fumio**. He ran a **Reiki** center in Shizuoka during **Usui Mikao**'s lifetime.

Okada Masayuki

He was a student of **Usui Mikao** and composed the text of Usui Mikao's **memorial stone** erected at the **Saihôji Temple** in Tôkyô in 1927 one year after the death of Usui Mikao.

O

Okudan

(Japanese) Innermost level.

Okuden

(Japanese) Inner teachings.

This is the name of **Level II** taught in most Japanese **branch**es of **Reiki**. **Hawayo Takata** was taught Okuden (she actually wrote

'Okudon' in her diary but her spelling of Japanese words was unreliable). The **Usui Reiki Ryôhô Gakkai** includes two grades within Okuden, one is called **zenki** and the other is **kôki**.

This Japanese term signifies that you have begun working at this **level** – it does not signify that you have completed the level.

Oneness

A concept where you become One with the universe. No separation, you are the Universe and the Universe is you. Oneness is absolute truth. To face oneness means to face everything – yourself, the world, every being, and everything - in its absolute truth.

Oneness is considered to be a characteristic of the mantra **HSZSN** and **Symbol 3**.

Onuki Yûji

A student of **Eguchi Toshihiro**. A Western Reiki teacher claimed to have met and studied with him in the 1970s in Morocco.

On Yomi

There are two methods of pronouncing Japanese **kanji**. One is on yomi where the Chinese reading and meaning are attached to the kanji. The other is **kun yomi**.

Oomoto Religion

Oomoto is the name of a **Shintô sect** con-sidered to be one of the **new religions** of Japan. An influential member was **Ueshiba Morihei** the founder of **aikidô**. It has been suggested that he knew **Usui Mikao**.

The true Reiki **mantra** of the pseudonym **CKR** is also used within the Oomoto religion. Oomoto have extracted it from the Shintô teachings.

A spokesman for Oomoto, Masamichi Tanaka, states that the true mantra (not the pseudonym) of CKR literally means "Direct Spirit" and that it is a part of the Divine Spirit which all of us are bestowed with from God, the Creator of the universe. He writes that, "This is a word (or term) we use at Oomoto and Shinto."

One more interesting point is that Oomoto appears to have no concern about writing or discussing the complete mantra with those outside the religion, unlike some within the system of **Reiki**. This attitude can help **Reiki practitioner**s to understand that it is not the mantra or **symbol** that is 'powerful' but rather the practitioner's personal work with them.

Open Heart Exercise
Non-traditional technique used to create a trusting and open relationship with others.

Oshite Chiryô Hô
(Japanese) A hand pressure **technique**.

P

Phaigh, Bethel (?-1986)

One of the 22 **Reiki Master** students of **Hawayo Takata**. She wrote two books, one called *Gestalt and the Wisdom of the Kahunas* and the other, *Journey into Consciousness* (unpublished). According to **Robert Fueston** she studied over a short period of time with Hawayo Takata and wrote in *Journey into Consciousness*, "The lessons (in life that I needed to learn) may have been particularly painful because my initiations had been timed so closely together. I had left Hawaii that spring not knowing of **Reiki**. I return this winter as a Reiki Master, a very green one."

Bethel Phaigh studied to become a Reiki Master after meeting **Barbara Brown** who told her all about Hawayo Takata. She died on 3 January 1986.

Photo Technique

This is a **technique** used to send **distant healing** and is based on the Japanese technique **enkaku chiryô hô**. A simple version of this is where a photo is held in the hands with the intent that **Reiki** be sent to who or whatever is in the photo.

Power Sandwich

Non-traditional technique said to increase effectiveness of **hands-on healing** or **distant healing** treatments.

Power Symbol

The name sometimes applied to **CKR** and **Symbol 1** in Western forms of the system of **Reiki**.

In Japan its characteristic is considered to be **Focus**.

Precepts

See **Five Precepts**

Protection

Some modern **branches of Reiki** claim that a **Reiki practitioner** must protect him or herself against the energy of others with certain **technique**s and practices. These are often developed with practices taken from the **New Age movement**.

It is true that we can affect one another with our energy and if someone wishes to do you harm energetically it might be possible. This is commonly called a **psychic attack**.

Traditionally it is taught that to protect oneself from outside influences one must be strong within. Therefore the most effective protection that the system of **Reiki** could offer a practitioner would be the ongoing practice of a technique like **hatsurei hô**. With this technique the practitioner's original energy strengthens, and offers a deeper awareness of energy. In this way the practitioner can sense what is happening and yet is not necessarily affected by it.

P

Proxy Methods

Proxy methods are Western **techniques** used to send **distant healing** and are based on the Japanese technique **enkaku chiryô hô**. There is the Knee method, Pillow method or Teddy Bear method. These items or parts of the body are used as a proxy for the individual that **Reiki** is being sent to. This concept attempts to help those who have difficulty setting clear **intent** when performing distant healing.

Psychic Attack

See **Protection**

Pure Land

Hônen brought Pure Land **Buddhism** to Japan. It is also known as **Jôdo Shû**. The goal of this Buddhist school is to be reborn in the Pure Land of **Amida Nyorai**. The main practice of Pure Land Buddhism is to recite Namu-Amida-Butsu, which is an expression of Oneness. Namu-Amida-Butsu translates as 'I take refuge in Amida Nyorai Buddha'.

Usui Mikao is buried in a Pure Land temple in Tôkyô and **Inamoto Hyakuten** believes that Usui Mikao belonged to this **sect**. According to some of the early teachings of Usui Mikao it is claimed that **Symbol 2** is connected to Amida Nyorai.

P

Q

Qi Gong

(Chinese) Energy cultivation.

This term refers to exercises that improve health and longevity as well as increase the sense of harmony within oneself and in the world. Japanese **ki ko technique**s are based on Qi Gong.

R

Rabinovitch, Prof. Judith

Professor Judith Rabinovitch. Ph.D., Harvard University; Currently Karashima Professor of Japanese Language and Culture Department of Foreign Languages and Literatures, University of Montana, USA.

She studied **Tenohira** ryôji with Miss Endo (an original student of **Eguchi Toshihiro**) for one week. "Miss Endo (then aged around 97 in 1994), an original **Ittôen** student of Eguchi Toshihiro ca 1929 or 1930. She initiated me without my knowing it, just by putting my hands under hers (I had no idea what for at the time) for a longish period of time and then telling me just to 'keep practicing', saying my hands were very good. This sort of informal **initiation** and a call for practice seems to have been the way at Ittôen."

Q
R

Professor J. Rabinovitch reports feeling great energy in her body and hands thereafter and continued to practice for 10 years. She went on to train through to the teacher level with a Japanese priest in 2002.

Professor J. Rabinovitch has copies of Eguchi Toshihiro's diaries and monographs and is interested in continuing her research into spiritual **healer**s from the early 1900s in Japan.

Radiance Technique, The

A **branch of Reiki** developed in the early 1980s. The founder, **Barbara Weber Ray** claims to be the only student of **Hawayo Takata** to have received the true teachings of the system of **Reiki**. She published a book called *The Reiki Factor* in 1983 where she describes three **level**s in the system but then goes on to change this in later editions to seven levels. This branch includes the **non-traditional** Japanese sounding **symbol**s of **Chi Ka So** and **Shi Ka Sai Ki**.

Raku

Non-traditional lightening-like **symbol** that is practiced in 'Tibetan' **branch**es **of Reiki**. It is used at the end of their **attunement**s and claims to separate the energies of the teacher and student.

Raku Kei Reiki

Iris Ishikuro, student of **Hawayo Takata**, and **Arthur Robertson** created this **branch of Reiki**. Together they had an immense impact on the future of the system of **Reiki**. They introduced a great deal of what is called 'Tibetan' information into the system.

This included the 'Tibetan' **symbol**s, the **Johre symbol,** and 'Tibetan' **technique**s such as **breath of the fire dragon** and the **hui yin breath**. Iris Ishikuro died in 1984.

R

Rama Symbol

Non-traditional symbol used in **Karuna Reiki®**, **Tera Mai™**, and **Karuna Ki**. It claims to clear the mind, clear the room of negative energies, harmonize upper **chakra**s with lower chakras and create determination and completion. Originally **channel**ed by Kellie-Ray Marine from the USA who called the **symbol** Rama.

Ray, Barbara Weber

She became a **Reiki Master** with **Hawayo Takata** on 1 September 1979. She studied **Level 1** in August 1978 and **Level II** in October 1978.

Harry Kuboi, another master student of Hawayo Takata, said she had sent him a letter stating that if he wanted to become a certified Reiki Master he would have to re-train with her and pay several thousand dollars.

She founded the American Reiki

Association in 1980 (now called the American-International Reiki Association) and **The Radiance Technique**.

She wrote a book in 1983 called *The Reiki Factor* that later changed its name to *The Reiki Factor in The Radiance Technique*. In the later editions of this book she states there are seven **level**s in the system of **Reiki**. The first edition notes that there are just three levels (the same as Hawayo Takata's other Reiki Master students).

Re-Attune

Some teachers claim to be able to re-attune you. As an **attunement** is a clearing of the body's energy it is impossible to be able to undo this or 'wipe-it-out'. Each attunement received takes the student a step further to realigning oneself with the natural function of the body – either mentally, physically, emotionally or spiritually.

Reido Reiki

A fusion between Japanese and Western forms of **Reiki** which was founded by Aoki Fuminori. It includes a **non-traditional symbol** called the **Koriki**.

Reiha

(Japanese) Wave of rei.

According to the 1933 book *Reiki To Jinjutsu–Tomita Ryû Teate Ryôhô* (*Reiki and Humanitarian Work–Tomita Ryû Hands Healing*) by **Tomita Kaiji**, a student of **Usui Mikao**, it describes the tingling sensation that is comparable to an electrical current. The heat created and the wave of rei are what he believed constituted spiritual energy.

Reiji Hô

(Japanese) Being guided by spirit **technique**.

Reiju

(Japanese) Spiritual Blessing.

This is the Japanese name for **attunements/ initiations/transformations**. Reiju is one of the **five elements of the system of Reiki**. Reiju helps to strengthen students' connection with spiritual energy and raises their personal energy levels. This in turn gives a sense of reconnection to one's true self. It also helps to clear the **meridians** allowing students to conduct more energy through the body.

Reiju is just the first step. Students are also asked to practice with the mind and the body using the other four elements of the system of Reiki.

Reiju is the same for each **level** – there are no differences as it is the student's ability to draw on more energy that creates the differences not the reiju itself.

No **symbol**s or **mantra**s are used in the reiju. The reiju does not 'attune' the student to the symbols as is believed in the West. The reiju appears to have links to practices from within the more esoteric elements of **Tendai** called

Mikkyô. It mirrors a Tendai ritual called **go shimbô** also known as 'Dharma for Protecting the Body'.

The **ritual** of reiju supports the teacher in making the connection with the energy. If a teacher practices hard and long he or she will find that it will be possible to eventually leave the physicality of the ritual behind.

It is believed that **Usui Mikao** would just sit opposite the student and create an energetic space where the reiju could occur, there was no physical ritual involved or any use of mantras and symbols.

Eguchi Toshihiro, a student of Usui Mikao apparently also worked in this way. **Professor J. Rabinovitch** writes of her teacher "Miss Endo (then aged around 97 in 1994), an original **Ittôen** student of Eguchi Toshihiro ca 1929 or 1930. She initiated me without my knowing it, just by putting my hands under hers (I had no idea what for at the time) for a longish period of time and then telling me just to 'keep practicing', saying my hands were very good. This sort of informal initiation and a call for practice seems to have been the way at Ittôen."

A recently published Japanese book by Mihashi Kazuo on Eguchi Toshihiro's life also states that he said that everyone can do **hands-on healing** once it is opened up. The way to open it is to do **gasshô** and **meditate** and then someone with a stronger power connects with you. This is a good description of reiju. That 'stronger power' should be the teacher who has practiced the **technique**s for an extended period and knows how to connect strongly with the energy.

Reiki

R

(Japanese) Spiritual energy.

These two **kanji** represent the word 'Reiki' in Japanese. Reiki is the name of the energy that is used within the system of Reiki. It is the energy of everything.

Koyama Kimiko, former president of the **Usui Reiki Ryôhô Gakkai**, told her student **Doi Hiroshi** that, "Reiki is the light of love".

To find out about the Japanese pronunciation of Reiki see **Leiki**.

Reiki (The System of)

This system has its origins in the early 1900s. It is believed that it was heavily influenced at that time by **Tendai**, **Mikkyô**, **Shugendô**, **Shintô** and the general popularity of spiritual and **healing** systems that were blossoming at that time.

There are **five elements of the system of Reiki**. They are that every student receives **attunement**s or **reiju**, and learns about **hand position**s, the **precepts**, **symbol**s and **mantra**s (from **Level II** onward), and **meditation**s and/or **technique**s.

It is believed that **Usui Mikao** did not call his teachings by this name. The word 'Reiki' appeared often in conjunction with his teachings but this was merely to point out that the teachings worked with Reiki ie. spiritual energy. Once his teachings came to the West in 1938 they became known as Reiki, the system.

Professor J. Rabinovitch states that the terms 'rei' and 'reiki' in Japan at the turn of the 20th century "were of course widely known and had many meanings in the healing world, connoting spiritual matters/spiritual forces or various sorts."

Reiki Alliance, The

An organization formed by some of **Hawayo Takata**'s Master students after her death in 1980. In 1982 they all came together, according to Carel Anne Farmer, and compared **symbols** and **mantras** (and **attunements** according to **John Harvey Gray**). They were surprised when they found that they differed. This group then standardized these elements of the system of **Reiki**.

Hawayo Takata's granddaughter, **Phyllis Lei Furumoto**, was named as their

Grandmaster and **lineage** bearer – the first time that these words had ever been used by anyone in conjunction with the system of **Reiki**.

The Reiki Alliance maintains a requirement that the Master Level should cost $10,000. An attempt was made by Phyllis Lei Furumoto in the 1990s to trademark words like 'Reiki', which failed in most countries except South America.

Reiki Aura Cleansing
Non-traditional technique for **clearing** the **aura** of 'heavy' energy.

Reiki Boost
Non-traditional technique that balances and harmonizes the **chakra**s allowing a greater flow of **Reiki** in the body. Also called the quick treatment, and the preparative mini Reiki session.

Reiki Box

Non-traditional technique to send **Reiki** to a person, place or event in the past, present or future. A list is written up, placed in a box and Reiki is offered to it.

Reiki Circle

A coming together of **Reiki practitioners** where **group Reiki** is practiced.

Reiki Course

Traditionally there are three **levels** in the system of **Reiki**. By studying a Reiki course the student begins to work at that level. The **five elements of the system of Reiki** will be experienced at each of the levels, with the student gradually discovering them in greater depth as he or she progresses.

Reiki Guide Meditation

Non-traditional technique to meet your **Reiki guide**.

Reiki Guides

The concept of guides is an add-on to the system of **Reiki**. It might stem from shamanism yet witches were also known to have familiars. Mystics, too, have been guided throughout the centuries by **angel**ic beings – so the concept of spiritual guidance is quite broad based. It has been popularized in the modern Reiki system.

Reiki Jin Kei Do

A practice inspired by the system of **Reiki** that includes Indian and Tibetan teachings. It also holds an unverified alternative history of the system of **Reiki** and teaches a **non-traditional symbol** called the **Buddho symbol**.

Reiki Master

Someone who has completed **Level III** or **Shinpiden** and is allowed to teach other people the system of **Reiki**. The title might not necessarily mean that this individual can guide you on your spiritual path or even understands the concept of Reiki. Some branches may only teach the **attunement** to their teacher students while others may offer an extensive training. The minimal requirement to become a Reiki Master in the West is that you know how to perform the attunement.

Reiki Master/Practitioner

A title developed in the West for someone who has completed only half of the third **level** of the system of **Reiki**. This is a new innovation. It means that the student has not learnt the **attunement** only the fourth **mantra** and **symbol**. Commonly used in the 'Tibetan' **branch**es **of Reiki**.

R

Reiki Master/Teacher

A title used in the West for two different purposes. One is to signify that the student has completed both **level**s of a form of Reiki where the third level is split in two. See **Reiki Master/Practitioner**.

The second purpose is that many **Reiki Masters** today do not believe that the term 'Master' is relevant as a description of what they do. There is the suggestion that it is arrogant to call yourself a 'Master' after what is generally a brief course. The title Master/Teacher is meant to suggest that the person is in fact a teacher rather than a guru of some sort.

Although the name Reiki Master is an accepted term in the West for a Reiki teacher perhaps it is good to keep this quote from Yukiyoshi Takamura (1928-2000) in mind "Anyone who refers to himself as a 'master', isn't".

Reiki Mawashi

(Japanese) A current of spiritual energy.

Reiki Meditation

Non-traditional meditation using **Reiki** to increase sensitivity and connection to the source.

Reiki Practitioner

Anyone who has completed a minimum of **Level I** in the system of **Reiki**.

If one wishes to practice professionally then it is suggested that **Level II** be first completed. **Usui Mikao** is quoted in the *Reiki Ryôhô Hikkei* as saying, "If you can't heal yourself, you can't heal others".

In the West the name also indicates someone who gives **Reiki treatment**s to others.

Reiki Ryôhô Hikkei

(Japanese) Spiritual Energy Method Manual.

The *Reiki Ryôhô Hikkei* is a 68-page document divided up into four sections. The cover of the manual is included here. There is the introduction or explanation by **Usui Mikao**; a question and answer section with Usui Mikao; the *Ryôhô Shishin* or healing guide with specific hand positions and 125 **gyosei** (poetry of the **Meiji Emperor**).

It was given to **Shoden (Level 1)** students

of the **Usui Reiki Ryôhô Gakkai**.

General thought today has it that **Hayashi Chûjirô** largely created the healing guide for Usui Mikao.

Koyama Kimiko, former president of the Usui Reiki Ryôhô Gakkai, compiled the *Reiki Ryôhô Hikkei* for the society's fiftieth anniversary from past Usui Reiki Ryôhô material. Therefore, although the *Reiki Ryôhô Hikkei* has been promoted as **Usui Mikao**'s manual, it was not written by him.

Reiki Salad

Hawayo Takata was renowned for her 'Reiki Salad' as she called it. Some of her recommended recipes for better health included sunflower seeds, red beet, grape juice and almonds. Two students of **Virginia Samdahl**'s wrote a book in 1984 called *The Reiki Handbook*, which included Reiki recipes.

Reiki Shares

See **Reiki Circle**.

Reiki Shower

Non-traditional cleansing technique that also increases energy flow in the body.

Reiki Stacks

Non-traditional Western **technique** used for sending **distant Reiki**. This is similar to the technique **Reiki box** and the **healing list**s where lists are written up and **Reiki** is offered to them.

Reiki Teacher

A **Reiki Master** that does not wish to use the word 'Master' due to its implications of having perfected working with spiritual energy. See also **Reiki Master/Teacher**.

Reiki Treatment

Reiki treatments come in all shapes and sizes. A treatment can be performed on the self or on others. In this photo someone is receiving a Reiki treatment while sitting in **seiza**. It is taken from **Tomita Kaiji**'s book published in 1933; he was a student of **Usui Mikao**.

If working on others, the **client** lies or sits and the **Reiki practitioner**'s hands are placed on or just above the body. It is unnecessary for the client to remove one's clothes and no private parts of the body should be touched. There is no place for sexual contact or inference within the system of **Reiki**. The practitioner **channels** energy through his/her body and the client draws what he/she requires at that point in time.

The treatment may take from about five minutes to an hour. Reiki treatments may also be used as a form of **first aid**. See also **Self-treatment** and **Hand Positions**.

Reiki Undô

(Japanese) Movement of spiritual energy **technique**.

Reizan-in Shuyo Tenshin Koji

Usui Mikao's posthumous Buddhist name (called **kaimyô** in Japanese).

Inamoto Hyakuten states that this is a typical **Pure Land** Buddhist name.

R

Ritual

Within the system of **Reiki** a number of rituals are practiced. Ritual is in place to teach us the groundrules and direct us. Once we know and understand these rituals it is time for us to free ourselves of them and move to integration or **Oneness** with the true meaning of the practice. This may take many years or even a whole life time. In fact a **Reiki practitioner** may never reach the stage where he/she can fully detach from the need for ritual.

All **five elements of the system of Reiki** can be seen as rituals. They are the practicing of **attunement** or **reiju**, **symbol**s and **mantra**s, **precepts**, **hand position**s, and **technique**s and **meditation**s.

Ritual could be described as 'the raft' of which the Vietnamese Buddhist Thich Nhat Hahn writes in his commentaries on the Diamond **Sutra**,

"The raft is to help us cross over to the other shore. It is a wonderful, even necessary instrument. But we should use the raft in an intelligent way. We should not cling to it or carry it on our back after we have done with it. The teaching is to help us, not to be possessed by us. It is not meant to deceive us, but we may be deceived by it because of our own way of clinging to it."

Professor J. Rabinovitch writes of this when explaining the views of **Eguchi Toshihiro**, a student of **Usui Mikao**. She draws her understandings from Eguchi Toshihiro's diaries, "One important thing to bear in mind is that Eguchi did not have many 'methods' of the modern sort to speak of and in his writing plainly states that people with methods start to rely on those as though it is the 'method' that leads to **healing**, when it is other deeper spiritual connections that bring healing."

Robertson, Arthur (?-2001)

He first studied with **Hawayo Takata**'s student, **Virginia Samdahl** in 1975. He then went on to study and work with another of Hawayo Takata's students, **Iris Ishikuro**, in the early 1980s. Together they created **Raku Kei Reiki**. Iris Ishikuro asked Arthur Robertson never to charge $10,000 for a Reiki Master class but to make it more affordable for people. In a 1983 Raku Kei Reiki manual the **non-traditional techniques** taught included the **breath of the fire dragon**, the **hui yin breath** and the **kanji hand mudras**. This appears to be the first time that they had been used in connection with the system of **Reiki**. Arthur Robertson also worked with Master Frequency Plates with an **antakharana** inside. These additions to the system of Reiki have made a profound impact on how it is taught today. Most of the 'Tibetan' systems have stemmed from Arthur Robertson's teachings. Arthur Robertson died in 2001.

Ryôhô

(Japanese) **Healing** method.

Ryôhô Shishin

(Japanese) **Healing** guide.

There are two healing guides that we are aware of. The first belongs within the **Usui**

Reiki Ryôhô Gakkai's larger manual called the *Reiki Ryôhô Hikkei*. The other is from a later date and was written by **Hayashi Chûjirô** for his students. They contain almost identical **hand position**s for treating specific illnesses. Due to their similarities it is guessed that **Usui Mikao** requested that Hayashi Chûjirô write the

R

first healing guide too as he was a qualified **doctor**.

It is uncertain when Hayashi Chûjirô first used his healing guide. The front cover of his healing guide (pictured here) reads *Ryôhô Shishin* and explains that it had been set up for American distribution. The branch name on the cover is the **Hayashi Reiki Kenkyû Kai** (Hayashi Spiritual Energy Research Society). It also states that it is not for sale and is a printed copy of the original. The actual manual is written in Japanese.

Hawayo Takata is known to have handed it to a number of her students including Harue Kanemitsu. **John Harvey Gray** also received a copy from **Alice Takata**, Hawayo Takata's daughter.

S

Sacred

The word sacred is often used to explain why some **Reiki practitioner**'s do not show their **symbol**s and **mantra**s to those who have not studied the appropriate levels of the system of **Reiki**. Some Reiki practitioners even believe that the symbols and mantras are secret.

For these reasons the *A-Z of Reiki* has used pseudonyms for the mantras instead. They are **CKR**, **SHK**, **HSZSN**, and **DKM**. The symbols are listed by their numbers from 1 to 4 as is taught in Japan and by their Western and Japanese characteristics.

Unbeknownst to many Western practitioners, in Japan some of the symbols and mantras are of use in the public arena and can be found today in martial arts, **Shintô**, martial arts and some **new religions**.

Saibo Kassei Kokyû

(Japanese) Vitalizing the cells through the breath **technique**.

Saihôji Temple

Pure Land Buddhist Temple in Tôkyô. The exact address is Toyotama district, 1-4-56 Umesato, Suginami Ku, Tôkyô. This is a photo of the entrance to the Temple grounds.

Here you can visit the **memorial stone** that was engraved by **Usui Mikao**'s students in 1927, one year after his death. **Okada Masayuki** composed it with brush strokes written by **Ushida Jûzaburô** in 1927. The memorial stone is one aspect of Usui Mikao's life as seen through the eyes of his students from the **Usui Reiki Ryôhô Gakkai**.

Sakoku

(Japanese) National isolation.

From 1639–1854, Japan was shut under a policy called 'sakoku' which had left it culturally prosperous though far behind the Western world technologically and militarily. Westerners were forbidden to enter Japan and trade. Only the Dutch were excluded. Through the small port of Dejima in Nagasaki the traders became Japan's single link to the West for more than two centuries. This privilege was only extended to contact with Japanese merchants and prostitutes.

Any Japanese who dared to venture abroad during this period were executed on their return to prevent any form of 'contamination'.

The **Meiji Emperor** (1852–1912) intro-

S

duced Japan to modernization and industrialization. **Christianity** was legalized in 1877.

Samdahl, Virginia (? -1994)

She was the first of **Hawayo Takata**'s 22 **Reiki Master** students. She received **Level I** in 1974, **Level II** in 1975 and became a Reiki Master in 1976. **Robert Fueston** states that he was told that Virginia Samdahl introduced **Barbara Weber Ray** to Hawayo Takata. This may account for the fact that after Hawayo Takata's death Virginia Samdahl was a member of two of the groups that claimed to carry on Hawayo Takata's teachings, one was **The Reiki Alliance** and the other was Barbara Weber Ray's **The Radiance Technique**. Virginia Samdahl retired from teaching Reiki in 1989 and died in 1994.

Samurai

(Japanese) Warrior.

Usui Mikao's family was **hatamoto** samurai – a high level within the ranks of samurai.

San

(Japanese) This is a neutral title, and can be used in most situations when addressing people.

In formal situations it may not be polite enough.

Sanskrit

An ancient Indian language created over 2000 years ago. It is the language of Hinduism, the Vedas and classical Indian literature but it is only used for religious purposes today. Some elements of **Buddhism** can be traced back to their Sanskrit origins.

The origin of the Japanese **symbol** called **kiriku** can be traced back to the Sanskrit **meditation** symbol called **hrih**. **Symbol 2** in the system of **Reiki** appears to be derived from the kiriku.

S

Sati Symbol

Non-traditional symbol used in **Tera Mai™**. It

is said to open, integrate and balance. Originally **channel**ed by Lawson Bracewall from New Zealand.

Satori

(Japanese) Spiritual enlightenment or awakening.

The method of attaining spiritual enlightenment would differ depending on which Buddhist **sect** you belonged to. Zen emphasized **meditation** as a means of experiencing awakening while the **Pure Land** sect uses the chanting of Namu-Amida-Butsu (I take refuge in **Amida Nyorai** Buddha).

Satya Reiki

A **branch of Reiki** that claims to be a non-western form of the system of **Reiki**. Largely taught in Pune, India and includes **technique**s such as **chakra balancing** and the **morning prayer**.

Scanning

Non-traditional technique sensing imbalances in the energy field.

Seated Chakra Treatment

Non-traditional technique stimulating the **chakra**s.

Sect

A small religious group that has branched off from a larger established group.

Seichim

A practice founded by Patrick Zeigler that was inspired by the system of **Reiki**. It originated with an experience he had in Egypt in the Great Pyramid in the King's chamber. It includes **symbol**s such as the **non-traditional** Japanese sounding **Cho Ku Ret**.

S

Seiheki Chiryô Hô

(Japanese) Treatment of mental patterns

technique.

This is the same treatment as **nentatsu hô** but with the inclusion of **mantra**s and **symbol**s.

Seishin Toitsu

(Japanese) Mental concentration.

This **technique** is also called **gasshô kokyû hô** and is a part of the technique **hatsurei hô**.

Seiza (1)

(Japanese) Correct sitting.

In this photo the man is sitting in **seiza** while meditating. It is taken from **Tomita Kaiji**'s book published in 1933; he was a student of **Usui Mikao**. This is a traditional Japanese style of sitting on top of the ankles, with the legs folded underneath and the back erect. It is a formal way of sitting on a tatami.

Sitting cross-legged is called agura which is more informal or casual. Seiza is used when you attend a formal occasion while agura would be used for informal occasions.

Seiza (2)

(Japanese) Sit still.

This is a different reading of the word seiza. It relates to a part of the **technique hatsurei hô** that can be found in the 1933 book, *Reiki To Jinjutsu–Tomita Ryû Teate Ryôhô* (*Reiki and Humanitarian Work–Tomita Ryû Hands Healing*) written by a student of **Usui Mikao** called **Tomita Kaiji**.

Sekizui Jôka Ibuki Hô

(Japanese) **Cleansing** the spinal cord with breath **technique**.

Self-healing

In the *Reiki Ryôhô Hikkei* **Usui Mikao** is asked the question, "If I can heal others, can I heal

myself?" His answer is, "If you can't heal yourself, how can you heal others?"
Self-healing is integral to all **Reiki** practices.

Self-Treatment

In this photo the woman is
performing a **Reiki treatment**
on herself while sitting in
seiza. It is taken from **Tomita
Kaiji**'s book published in
1933; he was a student of **Usui
Mikao**.

Reiki **practitioner**s place their hands on or
just off their own bodies, often in a structured
form, to support **self-healing**. See **Hand
Positions**.

Sensei

(Japanese) Teacher, master.

This is an honorific title, which people call
their teachers, doctors or any professional who
offers a service or instructions. In Japan the

founder of the system of **Reiki** is often referred to as Usui sensei.

As it is an honorific title it is inappropriate to call oneself sensei.

Seppuku

Suicide by disembowelment. **Hayashi Chûjirô** may have committed seppuku.

Serpent Fire Symbol

Non-traditional symbol taught in the 5th Level of the **Seven Level System**. The Seven Level System claims to be in the direct **lineage** of **The Radiance Technique** yet a very different **symbol** is taught at this level where it is called by the different name of **Chi Ka So**.

Seven Level System

The Seven Level System teachings are an off-shoot of **The Radiance Technique** which is a

break away from the Western teachings of
Hawayo Takata. However, The Radiance
Technique states that "Whatever is being
offered as '**Seven Level System**' has nothing to
do with The Radiance Technique." The Seven
Level System includes a number of **non–traditional symbol**s such as the Japanese sounding
symbol **Shi Ka Sai Ki**, **Serpent Fire Symbol**
and the **Gateway Symbol**.

Shakyo

(Japanese) **Sutra** Copying.

Sutras are copied by hand as a meditative
practice within **Tendai**. It is said that **Usui
Mikao**'s hand-copied sutras still exist on **hiei
zan** signed with the name **Gyoho**.

Shanti Symbol

Non-traditional symbol used in
Karuna Reiki®, **Tera Mai ™**, and
Karuna Ki. It is said to create trust,
heal insomnia, fear and panic and

manifest the best results. Originally **channel**ed by Pat Courtney from the USA.

Shihan

(Japanese) Instructor or teacher.

This term is used in some Japanese **lineage**s such as the **Usui Reiki Ryôhô Gakkai** and **Gendai Reiki Hô**.

Shi Ka Sai Ki

Non-traditional symbol taught in the 4th **level** of the **Seven Level System**. The Seven Level System claims to be in the direct **lineage** of **The Radiance Technique** yet a different **symbol** is taught at this level where it is called by the different name of Shi Ka Sei KI.

S

Shi Ka Sei Ki

Non-traditional symbol taught in the 4th **level** of **The Radiance Technique**.

Shiki

(Japanese) Way.

This word is used within the name of the **branch of Reiki** called **Usui Shiki Ryôhô** (Usui Way Healing Method).

Shinobu Saito

One of **Hawayo Takata**'s 22 **Reiki Master** students. She completed **Level 1** in 1976 and **Level II** in 1978, and became a Reiki Master in May 1980 in Palo Alto, California with Hawayo Takata. **Robert Fueston** states that Hawayo Takata hoped she would help take the system of **Reiki** back to Japan.

Shinpiden

(Japanese) Mystery teachings.

Japanese name for **Level III** or **Reiki Master** or **Reiki Master/Teacher**. **Hawayo Takata** was taught Shinpiden (she actually wrote 'Shinpeten' in her diary in 1936 but her spelling of Japanese words was unreliable) and the **Usui Reiki Ryôhô Gakkai** use the term too.

This Japanese term signifies that you have begun working at this **level** – it does not signify that you have completed the level.

Shintô
(Japanese) The way of the kami (gods).

Shintô is the indigenous faith of the Japanese people, and it is as old as the culture itself. The kami, or gods, are the objects of worship in Shintô. It has no founder and no sacred scriptures like the **sutra**s or the bible. Initially, it was so unselfconscious that it also had no name. The term, Shintô, came into use after the sixth century when it was necessary to distinguish it from the recently imported **Buddhism**.

It is not unusual for Japanese people to be followers of both Buddhism and Shintô. Today many people visit Shintô shrines for self-purification services. Purification rites are a vital part of Shintô.

A personal purification rite is the purifica-

S

tion by water; this may involve standing under a waterfall, which is known as **misogi**.

In **Usui Mikao**'s traditional teachings there is a **technique** called **kenyoku hô**, which is a kind of **misogi**. The use of **jumon** or **kotodama** is an aspect of Shintô that is also reflected in Usui Mikao's teachings.

Shiori

(Japanese) Guide, usually for beginners.

It is also known as the *Reiki Ryôhô No Shiori*. This is a booklet exclusively for members of the **Usui Reiki Ryôhô Gakkai** and was written by **Wanami Hôichi** and **Koyama Kimiko**, both presidents of the Usui Reiki Ryôhô Gakkai.

It consists of: the purpose, history and administrative system of the Usui Reiki Ryôhô Gakkai and includes the names of 11 of the 21 **Shinpiden** students taught by **Usui Mikao**; how to strengthen Reiki and includes **technique**s such as **byôsen reikan hô**, **gedoku**

hô, **kôketsu hô** and **nentatsu hô**; a teaching
from Usui Mikao; a guide to treatment;
characteristics of the Reiki healing method;
remarks by medical doctors and an explanation
of the **Ryôhô Shishin** (*Healing Guide*).

Shirushi

(Japanese) **Symbol**.

SHK

As the traditional **mantra**s of the system of
Reiki are considered as **sacred** by many,
pseudonyms are used in the *A-Z of Reiki* rather
than the true mantras. The pseudonym for the
second **traditional** mantra is the initials SHK.

The main Western characteristic of SHK is
mental/emotional and it is spoken three times in
conjunction with **Symbol 2**.

The main Japanese characteristic is
Harmony. In Japan, the mantra is not
necessarily used in conjunction with the
symbol. The early teachings of **Usui Mikao**

claim that SHK develops a **Reiki practitioner**'s link to the energy of **Heaven**.

Shodan
(Japanese) Beginner's level.

Shoden
(Japanese) First teachings.

This is the Japanese name for **Level I**. **Hawayo Takata** was taught Shoden (she actually wrote 'Shodon' in her diary but her spelling of Japanese words was unreliable) and the **Usui Reiki Ryôhô Gakkai** use the term too.

This Japanese term signifies that you have begun working at this **level** – it does not signify that you have completed the level.

Shogun
(Japanese) A General.

Shûchû Reiki

(Japanese) Concentrated spiritual energy.

Also called **shûdan Reiki**. This is what is called **group Reiki** in the west.

Shûdan Reiki

(Japanese) Group spiritual energy.

Also called **shûchû Reiki**.

Shugendô

(Japanese) The path of training and testing.

En-no-Gyoja is the legendary founder of this esoteric form of **Buddhism**. For 30 years from the year 666, En-no-Gyoja practiced in the mountains gaining him miraculous powers.

Shugendô practitioners were called **shugenja**.

Shugendô is a mix of shamanism, Taoism, Buddhism and **Shintô**. In fact Shugendô was outlawed around 1870 by the **Meiji Emperor**'s regime because of this typical scenario of the combination of specifically Buddhist and

S

Shintô elements. The government wanted a separation between Shintô and Buddhism which had become interwoven. The distinction between religions supported the Meiji regime in creating of Shintô a state religion. This unifying action promoted patriotisim in Japan. Shugenja were therefore made to choose which sect to belong to: Buddhist (either Tendai or Shingon) or Shintô.

Shugenja

(Japanese) Someone who practises **Shugendô**.

Also known as **yam-abushi**. Included is a photo of a yamabushi from the Shingon Buddhist sect. These were the 'mountain men' who were able to draw on the power of the kami (gods) through their magical powers aquired by esoteric practices. Shugenja would often heal disease, offer religious services, perform divination, exorcism and obtain oracles.

It is claimed that **Usui Mikao** was a shugenja.

Shûgyô

(Japanese) Deep mind /body training.

Shûgyô is a training performed in pursuit of deeper levels of consciousness. It is usually quite demanding, requiring unlimited amounts of effort, mindfulness and refinement.

Usui Mikao performed a form of shûgyô on **kurama yama**.

Shûyô Kai

(Japanese) Group meetings.

Shûyô means to cultivate one's mind or improve oneself. Shûyô kai was the name the **Usui Reiki Ryôhô Gakkai** once gave to their group meetings. After the shûyô kai there was the **jisshû kai**, the practical gathering, where some **technique**s were performed. Today the

Usui Reiki Ryôhô Gakkai group meeting is called the **kenkyû kai**.

Six Point Meditation for Energy Awareness

Non-traditional technique creating an even flow of energy in the body.

SKHM

This is the latest version of **Seichim**.

Smudging

Non-traditional technique using the vibration of smell to affect energy.

Solar Image Training

Non-traditional technique to aid in letting go of dependency on **symbol**s.

Sôsho

(Japanese) **Kanji** in modern, cursive style.

This is a kind of simplified shorthand that is

drawn according to asthetic standards.

Sôtô Zen
One of the two most important schools of Zen **Buddhism** in Japan. The **zazen shikan taza meditation** which **Doi Hiroshi** states may have been practised by **Usui Mikao** is heavily stressed in this school.

Stagnant energy
Universal energy flows through each and everything in life.

The human body has the ability to create obstacles to this natural flow. When the energy is not flowing in accordance with the natural flow, this is called stagnant energy.

The system of **Reiki** stimulates and strengthens energy flow in the body.

Sugano Wasaburo
Uncle of **Yamaguchi Chiyoko**. He lived in the North of Japan and studied **Reiki** with **Hayashi**

Chûjirô in 1928 in Sakai, Osaka. His motivation to learn Reiki came about due to the sense of helplessness he felt at the loss of his two childrens' lives.

It was Sugano Wasaburo who taught Yamaguchi Chiyoko how to perform an **attunement**.

Sutra

(Sanskrit) Rope or thread.

They are the records of religious texts.

Suzuki, Bizan

Author of a book called *Kenzen No Genri* (*The Principles of Health*) written in 1914. It includes similar **precepts** to those taught by **Usui Mikao**. A translation of this similar section in Bizan Suzuki's book is: "Today do not be angry, do not worry and be honest, work hard and be kind to people".

Another interesting fact is that the **kanji** for Bizan can be read as Miyama. Miyama cho is the modern name of Usui Mikao's town of origin.

Suzuki Sadako (?–1946)

Usui Mikao's wife. She died on 17 October 1946.

Her posthumous name on the gravestone is Te shin ing on ho jo ning dai shi.

Suzuki san (1895–)

It is said that Suzuki san is a **Tendai** nun who studied with **Usui Mikao** and is still alive today. She was a cousin of **Usui Mikao's** wife. Her formal training with him began in 1915 when she was 20 years old and her relationship with him continued on a less formal basis until his death in 1926. It is also said that she and a small number of other living students of Usui Mikao have preserved a collection of his papers from 1920 which includes **precepts**, **waka**, **meditation**s, and teachings.

The teachings which Suzuki san passes

down have no correlation to the system of **Reiki** other than that they originated with Usui Mikao. There are no **symbols** and **mantra**'s, no physical **attunement**s, a different set of precepts and no **handposition**s.

Symbol

Traditionally, there are four symbols in the system of **Reiki**. **Symbol**s 1 and 2 are clearly 'real' symbols while **3** and **4** are actual Japanese **kanji**. However anything can be used as a symbol and in this case the four symbols are extra tools whose purpose is to make it easier for students to practice the teachings.

They are **ritual**s that aid **Reiki practitioner**s in tapping into specific energy, although the symbols are not the energy themselves. You could see them as keys; insert them into the lock and open the door. Once that door is open and you have access to its contents you no longer need the key. Becoming attached to the key and constantly opening and closing the door means that you can never fully let go to enter and understand the contents of the room. Letting go of the symbols allows practitioners to move deeper into their connection with the energy but must not occur before the student is ready and the door is completely unlocked.

Doi Hiroshi has stated that **Usui Mikao** said, "As the symbols are the tools to connect with Reiki, they will be no longer needed when everything in your daily life comes to resonate with Reiki."

It is believed that only later in Usui Mikao's life, around 1923 (once he began working with lay people who were not involved in spiritual practices), were symbols introduced.

The names of the **traditional** Reiki symbols are **Symbol 1**, **2**, **3** and **4**. In the West the symbols are called by their accompanying **mantra**s rather than by numbers.

The symbols and mantras are considered **sacred** but in the West there is also a sense of forced secrecy around them. It is interesting to note that most of these mantras and symbols are openly discussed in Japan when they are used in martial arts, **Shintô**, and **new religions** unlike the system of Reiki (hence the need for pseudonyms in the *A-Z of Reiki*).

Reiki practitioners can learn from this Japanese attitude to symbols and mantras to overcome what may be exaggerated Western mysticism. This Japanese perspective also supports the understanding that it is not the mantra or symbol that is 'powerful' but rather the strength of the practitioner's commitment to practice.

In the *A-Z of Reiki* there are a number of symbols and mantras. Those listed as **traditional** were introduced by Usui Mikao while those listed as **non-traditional** have been added to the system since 1980.

Symbol 1

This is the first **symbol** of Reiki taught in **Okuden** or **Level II**. It is known as the

Power Symbol in the West.

Symbol 2

This is the second **symbol** of Reiki taught in **Okuden** or **Level II**. It is known as the **Mental/Emotional Symbol** in the West.

Symbol 3

This is the third **symbol** of Reiki taught in **Okuden** or **Level II**. This symbol is not really a symbol but **kanji**. Its meaning is, "my original nature is a correct thought" or another translation taught by **Doi Hiroshi** is, "right consciousness is the origin of everything".

This is known as the **Distance Symbol** in the West.

S

Symbol 4

This is the fourth **symbol** of Reiki taught in **Shinpiden** or **Level III**. This symbol is not really a symbol but **kanji**. It means 'Great Bright Light'. This kanji is not used solely within **Usui Mikao**'s teachings. It can be found in some Japanese martial arts as well as in **Mikkyô**, **Shugendô,** and some of the **new religions** like Shunmei.

Symbol Exercises

Non-traditional techniques to increase your connection to **Reiki** by meditating on the **symbol**s.

T

Takata, Hawayo (1900–1980)

One of the Reiki Master students of **Hayashi Chûjirô**. Hawayo Takata was born in Hawaii and studied with Hayashi Chûjirô in Japan from 1936 to 1938. She brought Hayashi Chûjirô's teachings to the West.

For 40 years she offered treatments and taught people about the system she called **Reiki**. Before she died in 1980 she had taught 22 **Reiki Master**s to carry on her teachings, leaving the list of their names with her sister.

Taketomi Kanichi (1878–1960)

Third president of the **Usui Reiki Ryôhô Gakkai** and a Rear Admiral in the Japanese Navy. He became a member of the society in

T

1925 and was taught by **Usui Mikao**.

Talismans
Non-traditional technique of manifesting using an image as the focus.

Tamasura
Non-traditional symbol used in 'Tibetan' **branches of Reiki**. Said to be an antidote to fear.

Tanden
(Japanese) The abdomen below the navel.

Also called **hara**.

Tanden Chiryo Hô
(Japanese) Detoxifying and purifying **technique**.

Taniai
Birthplace of **Usui Mikao**. He was born on 15 August 1865 in this village in the Yamagata

county of the Gifu Prefecture, Japan. This village is now called Miyama cho.

Tatsumi (?–1996)

According to a Western **Reiki practitioner** he was a teacher student of **Hayashi Chûjirô**. Tatsumi, trained in 1927 to become a teacher.

Tatsumi is said to have been taught in a class with five other students. He learnt seven basic **hand position**s from **Hayashi Chûjirô** before 1931. These were formulated to cover specific acupuncture points on the body. Though Tatsumi had never taught these teachings he still had the paperwork. These included hand written notes from Hayashi Chûjirô's teachings and copies of the four traditional **symbol**s. Tatsumi did not appreciate the changes that Hayashi Chûjirô had made and finally left in 1931. Tatsumi died in 1996.

Teate

(Japanese) **Hands-on healing**.

This is the generic term used for the many forms of hands-on healing that took place during the 20th century in Japan. A variety of groups were practicing teate, with some of the teachings spreading worldwide. Tenrikyo, Johrei and Mahikari were just some of these. See also **Johrei Reiki**.

Technique

Techniques are one of the **five elements of the system of Reiki**.

Some of them originate in Japan and others have been introduced over the last 25 years in the West.

Tendai

Buddhist **sect** in Japan. **Usui Mikao** is said to have been a Tendai lay priest and to have studied on **hiei zan**, the main Tendai temple complex in Japan.

Tendai was brought to Japan by Saichô in the early ninth century and names Nagarjuna as its patriarch. Tendai practitioners' believe that the **Lotus Sutra** is Buddha's complete and perfect teachings.

There are five general areas taught in Tendai. They are the teachings of the Lotus **Sutra**; esoteric **Mikkyô** practices; **meditation** practices; **precepts**; and **Pure Land** teachings.

Tenohira

(Japanese) **Hands-on healing**.

This is a term for a structured form of hands-on healing.

Tenohira Ryôji Kenkyû Kai

(Japanese) Hand Healing Research Center.

Eguchi Toshihiro, a student and friend of

Usui Mikao, created this hands-on healing society. The photo shows Eguchi Toshihiro with his students during his teachings.

Tenon in

The Buddhist name for Mariko Obaasan, who it is claimed was a student of **Usui Mikao** from 1920-1926.

Tera-Mai™ Reiki and Tera-Mai™ Seichem

A **non-traditional** practice founded by Kathleen Milner that was inspired by the system of **Reiki**. It includes many **channel**led **symbol**s and **mantra**s. Some of the non-traditional symbols taught at this level are **Halu**, **Iava**, **Rama**, **Sati**, **Shanti**, and **Zonar**. Tera-Mai™ was influencial in the origins of **Karuna Reiki®**.

Three-Week Cleansing Process

The **cleansing** process is also known as a

healing crisis. It is a response to an **attunement**, **reiju** or **Reiki treatment**.

The body is attempting to remove toxins and re-balance and this can often be felt physically, emotionally, mentally or spiritually.

After an attunement it is often said that the student will undergo a 21-day cleansing process in which the student must practice **Reiki** to aid the process. Though this is likely to be a recent Western addition to Reiki it certainly has had its share of esoteric interpretations.

21-Day practices can also be found in Japanese forms such as **Shugendô** and **Tendai**. For example; traditional meditations, like the Buddhist hokkesen, are practiced for the duration of 21 days.

Basically the popularity of the three-week cleansing process concept can be put down to the fact that it is successful – it achieves its aim. That aim as far as the system of Reiki is concerned is to get people practicing. After practicing Reiki for three weeks students don't want to stop practicing – it feels too good!

Tibetan Reiki

Generic teachings that may include practitioners of **Usui/Tibetan Reiki**, Tibetan/Usui Reiki or Wei Chi Reiki. The inspiration for these teachings is likely to have originated from **Raku Kei Reiki**.

Tomita Kaiji

A student of **Usui Mikao**. He wrote a book called *Reiki To Jinjutsu– Tomita Ryû Teate Ryôhô (Reiki and Humanitarian Work–Tomita Ryû Hands Healing)* in 1933. The book was re-published in

1999 with the help of **Mochizuki Toshitaka**.

Included in Tomita Kaiji's book are case studies, the **technique hatsurei hô** (which includes the use of **waka**), **hand positions** for

specific illnesses. The name of his school was
Tomita Teate Ryôhô Kai and it taught four
levels **Shoden**, Chuden, **Okuden** and Kaiden.

Tomita Teate Ryôhô Kai

Name of the school created by **Tomita Kaiji**, a
student of **Usui Mikao**. In his school he used
four levels called **Shoden**, Chuden, **Okuden**
and Kaiden.

Toning

Non-traditional technique of using the voice
as a **healing** tool.

Traditional

This term is used in the *A-Z of Reiki* to represent
teachings that are directly related to the
Japanese origins of the system of **Reiki**.

T

Transformation

This word is often used to describe the Japanese
reiju and/or the Western **attunement** process.

Tsuboi Sonoo

Student of **Usui Mikao** according to **Doi Hiroshi**.

Twan Wanja

One of **Hawayo Takata**'s 22 **Reiki Master** students. She wrote *In the Light of a Distant Star: A Spiritual Journey Bringing the Unseen into the Seen* and her daughter Anneli has compiled a book called *Early Days of Reiki: Memories of Hawayo Takata*.

U

Uchite Chiryô Hô

(Japanese) Patting with the hands **technique**.

Ueshiba Morihei (1883–1969)

Founder of **aikidô**. Ueshiba Morihei is claimed to have been an acquaintance of **Usui Mikao**. Ueshiba Morihei taught **kotodama** in his method, not unlike Usui Mikao.

Ushida Jûzaburô (1865–1935)

Second president of the **Usui Reiki Ryôhô Gakkai**. He was also a Rear Admiral in the Japanese navy.

Ushida was taught by **Usui Mikao** and became a member of the society in 1925. Ushida Jûzaburû drew the brush strokes on Usui Mikao's **memorial stone** in 1927.

Usui Dô

(Japanese) The way of Usui.

Branch of Reiki that holds an unverified alternative history to the system of **Reiki**.

Usui Fuji (1908–1946)

Usui Mikao's son. He was a teacher at Tôkyô University.

Usui Mikao (1865–1926)

Usui Mikao is the founder of the system of **Reiki**. He was born on 15 August 1865, in the village of Taniai mura in the Yamagata district of the Gifu Prefecture, in Japan. His father's name was Uzaemon and they were from the **Chiba** clan.

There is very little reliable information available about Usui Mikao's life apart from the **memorial stone**. Much is still hearsay. This history is pieced together from various sources.

Usui Mikao is believed to have been a Buddhist and as a child studied in a **Tendai** monastery. He remained Tendai all his life and may have become a Tendai lay priest.

Usui Mikao married **Suzuki Sadako** and they had two children, a boy and a girl, called **Usui Fuji** and **Usui Toshiko** respectively. He is thought to have studied on **hiei zan** and practiced certain **meditation**s on **kurama yama**. It has been suggested that old **sutra** copies on **hiei zan** have Usui Mikao's Buddhist name or extra name of **Gyoho** or Gyotse on them.

It is said that Usui Mikao practiced **Shugendô** and that his teachings are founded in this practice of mountain **Buddhism**.

His teachings included using **waka**, the **five precepts**, **meditation**s and **technique**s, **mantra**s and/or **symbol**s, and **reiju**.

Professor J. Rabinovitch writes that, "Japan was in a great popular health movement from the teens onward and continuing well up

U

through the 30s, only hampered by Japan's entry into WWII. Hand healers, psychics, intuitives, and every imaginable kind of psychic healer plied their trades all around the country. However deeply respected and influential he was among his immediate **healer**-peers and disciples, Usui was but one island of **healing** activity."

The names of 11 of the 21 Master students of Usui Mikao have been recorded in a booklet used by the **Usui Reiki Ryôhô Gakkai**.

Usui Mikao's posthumous Buddhist name noted at the memorial stone site is **Reizan-in Shuyo Tenshin Koji.**

Usui Reiki

Generic term that is used by **Reiki practitioners** of a form of **Usui Shiki Ryôhô**. All **Reiki** stems back to the founder **Usui Mikao**, therefore all Reiki is Usui Reiki. This term does not qualify what is taught in this branch. To be considered a **branch of Reiki** it should include the **five elements of the system of Reiki**.

Usui Reiki Ryôhô

(Japanese) Usui Spiritual Energy Healing Method.

Hawayo Takata referred to the system of **Reiki** she learned from **Hayashi Chûjirô** as **Usui Reiki Ryôhô** in a recording in 1979. Her **certificate**s call it **Usui Shiki Ryôhô**.

The **memorial stone**, erected by early members of the Usui Reiki Ryôhô Gakkai, called the teachings Reiki Ryôhô.

There is also a **branch of Reiki** called Usui Reiki Ryôhô. It attempts to trace the history of the system of Reiki basing its principles on what **Usui Mikao** taught.

Usui Reiki Ryôhô Gakkai

(Japanese) Society of the Usui Spiritual Energy Healing Method.

The Usui Reiki Ryôhô Gakkai claims to have been created by **Usui Mikao** in 1922. The society still exists today, and has its seventh president.

It includes no foreigners in its ranks and members are asked not to discuss the details of the society with non-members. When this society was first started members of the Japanese navy largely attended it. There were once 80 divisions of the Usui Reiki Ryôhô Gakkai throughout Japan but today there are, at the most, five with the teachings taking place in Tôkyô. The society does not advertise and has not actively made contact with Westerners apart from one member **Doi Hiroshi**.

Doi Hiroshi has told about his experience of the meetings, **kenkyû kai,** held by former president **Koyama Kimiko** in the 1990s when she visited Kyôto once a month. The members would sit in a circle (on chairs rather than in **seiza**). Koyama **sensei** would talk about various topics based on her life experiences. The **gyosei** were recited followed by **kenyoku hô, jôshin kokyû hô** and **gasshô**. This was followed by

seishin toitsu as all members received **reiju**. Koyama sensei and one of the **shihan**s performed reiju. There was then a three time recitation of the **five precepts**, **reiji**, answers to questions, **Reiki mawashi** and **shûchû Reiki**.

There are three major **level**s in the Usui Reiki Ryôhô Gakkai. These are **Shoden**, **Okuden** and **Shinpiden** (the teacher level). Within these levels there are six grades of proficiency. Each member is supplied with the *Reiki Ryôhô Hikkei* and *shiori*.

Here is a list of presidents from Usui Mikao to modern day:

- **Usui Mikao** (1865–1926)
- **Ushida Jûzaburô** (Rear Admiral, 1865–1935)
- **Taketomi Kanichi** (Rear Admiral, 1878–1960)
- **Watanabe Yoshiharu** (Schoolteacher, ?–1960)
- **Wanami Hôichi** (Vice Admiral, 1883–1975)

U

- Koyama Kimiko (1906–1999)
- **Kondô Masaki** (University Professor)

Usui Shiki Ryôhô

(Japanese) Usui Way **Healing** Method.

Hawayo Takata used this name on the **certificate**s she issued. There are a number of **branch**es **of Reiki** that use the term Usui **Shiki** Ryôhô and yet there are variations in the teachings. **The Reiki Alliance**, **Phyllis Lee Furumoto**, **Beth Gray** and other teachers have used this name to represent their teachings. Today the majority of **Reiki practitioner**s state that they teach **Usui Reiki** or the Usui Natural System of Healing. By these terms they are referring to aspects of Usui Shiki Ryôhô in one of its many forms.

Usui Teate

(Japanese) **Hands-on healing** by **Usui Mikao**.

According to the **memorial stone** Usui Mikao was a well known hands-on **healer**. In the last four years of his life he began to teach **naval officers** how to heal themselves and others. This is claimed to have been to support them and their crews as a form of **first aid** while out on their vessels.

Hayashi Chûjirô, one of these naval officers, was also a **doctor** and he began what is often thought of as the first professional Reiki clinic. It is from his practice that the system of **Reiki** in the West has evolved.

Usui/Tibetan Reiki
See **Tibetan Reiki**.

Usui Toshiko (1913–35)
Usui Mikao's daughter.

U

V

Vajra Reiki

A Western practice inspired by the system of **Reiki**. It was largely influenced by **Johrei Reiki** and **Raku Rei Reiki.**

Violet Breath

Non-traditional breath **technique** used in **New Age movement** forms of the system of **Reiki** with the **attunement** process. This is very similar to the technique **breath of the fire dragon**.

Waka

(Japanese) Japanese verse.

The word waka is made up of two parts: 'wa' meaning 'Japanese' and 'ka' meaning 'poem' or 'song'.

Waka is a short form of poetry that contains 31 syllables. In English it is typically divided into five lines of 5,7,5,7 and 7 syllables.

In the 13th century in Japan, people began to believe that **waka** achieved supernatural effects because they were **darani** or spells.

Waka, as written by the **Meiji Emperor**, is one of the components of **Usui Mikao**'s teachings.

The waka Usui Mikao used in his teachings are written down in the *Reiki Ryôhô Hikkei*, a manual used by the **Usui Reiki Ryôhô Gakkai**.

Tomita Kaiji, a student of Usui Mikao,

V
W

wrote in his 1933 book that the **technique hatsurei hô** included the student becoming One with the essence of the waka.

Eguchi Toshihiro, a friend and student of Usui Mikao, also used the Meiji Emperor's waka in his teachings according to the author Mihashi Kazuo.

It was a popular cultural social interaction at the turn of the 20th century and was very common among well-educated sections of the population.

Wanami Hôichi (1883–1975)

Fifth president of the **Usui Reiki Ryôhô Gakkai** who was taught by **Ushida Jûzaburô**. He was also a Vice Admiral in the Japanese navy.

Watanabe Yoshiharu (? -1960)

Fourth president of the **Usui Reiki Ryôhô Gakkai** who was taught by **Usui Mikao**. He was a Professor at the Takaoka

Commercial High School.

Water Ritual
Non-traditional technique of changing water into energized **healing** water.

Y

Yamabushi

(Japanese) Those who sleep in the mountain.

These are practitioners of **Shugendô**, also called **shugenja**. They live in the mountains and engage in ascetic practices.

Yamaguchi Chiyoko
(1920/21–2003)

Yamaguchi Chiyoko was taught **Levels I** and **II** by **Hayashi Chûjirô** in 1938. She said that she learnt both **Shoden** and **Okuden** together over five consecutive days.

Many of her family members were **Reiki practitioner**s and it was her uncle **Sugano Wasaburo** that taught her how to perform the **attunement**.

Her student **Inamoto Hyakuten** teaches **Komyo Reiki Kai**, inspired by her teachings. **Yamaguchi Tadao**, her son, teaches a branch of **Reiki** called **Jikiden Reiki** also based on her teachings.

Yamaguchi Tadao

Son of **Yamaguchi Chiyoko** and the founder of **Jikiden Reiki**. He has recently co-written a book about **Hayashi Chûjirô**. He has also been the Secretary General of a new religious group named Sekai Kyusei-kyo, founded by Okada Mokichi (1882-1955). Sekai Kyusei-kyo performs Johrei **healing**. For more information about Johrei see **Johrei Reiki**.

Yamashita, Kay

One of **Hawayo Takata**'s sisters and trained by Hawayo Takata as a **Reiki Master**.

Yuri in (1897–1997)

It is claimed that this Buddhist nun studied **Usui Mikao**'s teachings alongside **Tenon in** from 1920–1926.

Z

Zaike

(Japanese) Lay priest.

A lay priest resides in his own home, not in a monastery. **Usui Mikao** is said to have been a **Tendai** zaike.

Zazen Shikan Taza

A **Tendai meditation** practice that was supposedly practiced by **Usui Mikao** on **kurama yama**. For a complete version of this practice see *The Reiki Sourcebook*.

Zenki

(Japanese) First stage.

The first part or grade within **Okuden**.

Zenshin Kôketsu hô

(Japanese) Whole body blood exchange.

Also called **ketsueki kôkan hô**. **Hawayo Takata** taught this as the **finishing treatment** or **nerve** stroke in her **Level 2** classes. By this inclusion it is apparent that she knew some of the more **traditional** Japanese **technique**s.

Zonar Symbol

Non-traditional symbol taught in **Karuna Reiki®**, **Tera Mai™**, and **Karuna Ki**. It is said to heal past life issues and child abuse, and is connected to **Archangel** Gabriel. This was the first symbol **channel**ed by Kathleen Milner and Marcy Miller.

Zui-Un

(Japanese) Auspicious cloud.

The name (not **mantra**) of **Symbol 1** taught in **Komyo Reiki Kai**.

Bibliography

Abé, Ryûichi. *The Weaving of Mantra*, Columbia University Press, New York, 1999.

Arnold, Larry and Sandy Nevius. *The Reiki Handbook*, Psi, Oregon, 1992.

Barnett, Libby. *Reiki Energy Medicine: Bringing the Healing Touch into Home, Hospital and Hospice*, Healing Arts Press, Vermont, 1996.

Bary De, WM Theodore. *Sources of Japanese Tradition*, Columbian University Press, New York, 2001.

Blacker, Carmen. *The Catalpa Bow–A Study of Shamanic Practices in Japan*, Japan Library, Richmond, 1999.

Bracy, John and Liu Xing-Han. *Ba Gua–Hidden Knowledge in the Taoist Internal Martial Art*, North Atlantic Books, Berkeley, 1998.

Breen, John and Mark Teeuwen. *Shinto in History–Ways of the Kami*, Curzon Press,

B
I
B
L
I
O
G
R
A
P
H
Y

Surrey, 2000.

Brown, Fran. *Living Reiki–Takata's Teachings*, Life Rhythm, California. 1992.

Chadwick, David. *Thank You and Ok! An American Zen Failure in Japan*, Penguin Books, London, 1994.

Chadwick, David. *The Life and Zen Teachings of Shunryu Suzuki*, Thorsons, London, 1999.

Cleary, Thomas. *The Japanese Art of War-Understanding the Culture of Strategy*, Shambhala Publications, Boston, 1991.

Cohen, Kenneth S. *The Way of Qi Gong*, Ballatine Books, New York, 1997.

Davey, H.E. *Living the Japanese Arts & Ways*, Stone Bridge Press, Berkeley, 2003.

Davey, H.E. *Japanese Yoga-The Way of Dynamic Meditation*, Stone Bridge Press, Berkeley, 2001.

Doi, Hiroshi. *Modern Reiki Method for Healing*, Fraser Journal Publishing, British Columbia, 2000.

Ellis, Richard. *Practical Reiki–Focus Your*

Body's Energy for Deep Relaxation and Inner Peace, Sterling Publishing Company, New York, 1999.

Floyd, H. Ross. *Shintô: The Way of Japan*, Greenwood Publishing Group, Westport, 1965.

Funakoshi, Gichin. *Karate-dô–My Way of Life*, Kodansha America Inc, New York, 1975.

Gaia, Laurelle Shanti. *The Book on Karuna Reiki–Advanced Healing Energy for Our Evolving World*, Infinite Light Healing Studies Center, Colorado, 2001.

Gleinsner, Earlene F. *Reiki in Everyday Living*, Jaico Publishing House, Delhi, 1997.

Gordon, Andrew. *A Modern History of Japan: From Tokugawa Times to the Present*, Oxford University Press, Oxford, 2002.

Gray, John Harvey and Lourdes. *Hand to Hand-The Longest-Practicing Reiki Master Tells His Story*, Xlibris Corporation, 2002.

Groner, Paul. *Saicho–The Establishment of the Japanese Tendai School*, University of

Hawaii Press, Honolunu, 2000.

Haberly, Helen J. *Reiki–Hawayo Takata's Story*, Archedigm Publications, Maryland, 2000.

Hall, Mari. *Practical Reiki-A Practical Step by Step Guide to this Ancient Healing Art*, Thorsons, London, 1997.

Hall, Mari. *Reiki for Common Ailments-A Practical Guide to Healing*, Piatkus, London, 1999.

Hanh, Thich Nhat. *Opening the Heart of the Cosmos–Insights on the Lotus Sutra*, Paralax Press, Berkeley, 2003.

Hanh, Thich Nhat. *The Diamond that Cuts Through Illusion–Commentaries on the Prajnaparamita Diamond Sutra*, Paralax Press, Berkeley, 1992.

Hayashi, Chûjirô. *Ryôhô Shishin*, Japan.

Hitoshi, Miyake. *Shugendô-Essays on the Structure of Japanese Folk Religion*, The University of Michigan, Michigan, 2001.

Honervogt, Tanmaya. *The Power of Reiki–An Ancient Hands-On Healing System*, Henry

Holt and Company, Inc, New York, 1998.

Horan, Paula. *Abundance Through Reiki*, Windpferd, Aitrang, 1990.

Horan, Paula. *Core Empowerment*, Full Circle, Delhi, 1998.

Horan, Paula. *Exploring Reiki - 108 Questions & Answers*, New Page Books, New York, 2005.

Ikegami, Eiko. *The Taming of the Samurai: Honorific Individualism and the Making of Modern Japan*, Harvard University Press, Cambridge, 1995.

Inagaki, Hisao. *A Dictionary of Japanese Buddhist Terms*, Nagata Bunshodo, Kyoto, 2003.

Jahnke, Roger. *The Healing Promise of Qi*, Contemporary Books, New York, 2002.

Japanese Journals of Religious Studies, Nanzan Institute for Religion and Culture, Japan.

Jarell, David G. *Reiki Plus® Natural Healing*, Reiki Plus, Key Largo, 1997.

Keene, Donald. *Emperor of Japan–Meiji and

His World, 1852-1912, Columbia University
Press, New York, 2002.

Kelly, Maureen J. *Reiki and the Healing
Buddha*, Lotus Press, Twin Lakes, 2000.

LaFleur, William R. *The Karma of Words –
Buddhism and the Literary Arts in Medieval
Japan*, University of California Press, Los
Angeles, 1986.

Lubeck, Walter. *The Complete Reiki Handbook*,
Windpferd, Aitrang, 1990.

Lubeck, Walter. *Rainbow Reiki*, Lotus Light
Publications, Twin Lakes, 1997.

Lubeck, Walter., Frank Arjava Petter and
William Lee Rand. *The Spirit of Reiki*, Lotus
Press, Twin Lakes, 2001.

Lugenbeel, Barbara. *Virginia Samdahl-Reiki
Master Healer*, Grunwald and Radcliff, 1984.

McCarthy, Patrick and Yukio. Funakoshi
Gichin's Tanpenshu, International Ryukyu
Karate Research Society, Brisbane, 2002.

Mihashi Kazuo. *Tenohira-ga Byoki-o Naosu*,
Chuo Art Publishing Co., LTD. 2001.

Milner, Kathleen. *Reiki & Other Rays of Touch Healing*, 1994.

Mitchell, Paul David. *Reiki–The Usui System of Natural Healing (The Blue Book)*, Mitchel, Paul David, Idaho, 1985.

Mizutani, Osamu and Nobuku. *An Introduction to Modern Japanese*, Japan Times Ltd, Tôkyô, 1977.

Mochizuki, Toshitaka. *Iyashi No Te*, Tama Shuppan, Tôkyô, 1995.

Mochizuki, Toshitaka. *Chô Kantan Iyashi No Te*, Tama Shuppan, Tôkyô, 2001.

Musashi, Miyamoto translated by Thomas Cleary. *The Book of Five Rings*, Shambhala Publications, Boston, 1999.

Nishida, Tenko. *A New Road to Ancient Truth*, Horizon Press, New York, 1972.

Oda, Ryuko. *Kaji-Empowerment and Healing in Esoteric Buddhism*, Kineizan Shinjao-in Mitsumonkai, Japan, 1992.

Petter, Frank Arjava. *Reiki Fire*, Lotus Press, Twin Lakes, 1998.

Petter, Frank Arjava. *The Original Reiki Handbook of Dr. Mikao Usui*, Lotus Press, Twin Lakes, 1999.

Petter, Frank Arjava. *Reiki–The Legacy of Dr. Usui*, Lotus Light Publications, Twin Lakes, 1998.

Paramhans Swami Maheshwarananda. *The Hidden Power in Humans*, Ibera Verlag, Vienna, 2004.

Prasad, Kathleen, Elizabeth Fulton. *Animal Reiki-Using Energy to Heal the Animals in Your Life*, Ulysses Press, Berkeley, 2006.

Radha, Swami Sivananda. *Kundalini Yoga for the West*, Shambhala Publications, Boston, 1981.

Rand, William Lee. *Reiki-The Healing Touch*, Vision Publications, Michigan, 2000.

Rand, William Lee. *Reiki for a New Millennium*, Vision Publications, Michigan, 1998.

Ray, Barbara Weber. *The Reiki Factor-First Edition*, Exposition Press, New York, 1983.

Reader, Ian. *Religion in Contemporary Japan*, University of Hawaii Press, Hawaii, 1991.

Reed, William. *Ki–A Practical Guide for Westerners*, Japan Publications Inc, Tokyo, 1986.

Reiki Ryôhô Hikkei, Usui Reiki Ryôhô Gakkai, Japan.

Sargent, Jiho, *Asking About Zen-108 Answers*, Weatherhill, Inc. New York, 2001.

Saso, Michael. *Tantric Art and Meditation*, Tendai Education Foundation, Honolulu, 1990.

Shewmaker, Diane Ruth. *All Love–A Guidebook to Healing with Sekhem-Seichim Reiki and SKHM*, Celestial Wellspring, Olympia, 1999.

Steven, John. *Sacred Calligraphy of the East*, Shambhala Publications, Boston, 1996.

Steven, John. *The Marathon Monks of Mount Hiei*, Shambhala Publications, Boston 1988.

Stiene, Bronwen and Frans. *The Reiki Sourcebook*, O Books, Winchester, 2003.

Stiene, Bronwen and Frans. *The Japanese Art of Reiki*, O Books, Winchester, 2005.

Stein, Diana. *Essential Reiki–A Complete Guide to an Ancient Healing Art*, Crossing Press, Berkeley, 1995.

Suzuki, D.T. *Buddha of Infinite Light–The Teachings of Shin Buddhism, The Japanese Way of Wisdom and Compasion*, Shambhala Publications, Boston, 1998.

Suzuki, D.T. *Manual of Zen Buddhism*, Rider & Company, London, 1986.

Suzuki, Shunryu. *Zen Mind, Beginners Mind*, Weatherhill, New York, 1970.

Suzuki, Shunryu. *Branching Streams Flow in the Darkness: Lectures on the Sandokai*, University of California Press, Berkeley, 1999.

Suzuki, Shunryu, *Not Always So-Practicing the True Spirit of Zen*, HarperCollins, New York, 2002.

Takata Furumoto, Alice. *The Gray Book*, Takata Furumoto, Alice, 1982.

Tanabe, George J. Jr. *Religions of Japan in Practice*, Princeton University Press, Princeton, 1999.

Tohei, Koichi. *Ki in Daily Life*, Ki-no-Kenkyûkai, Tôkyô, 1980.

Tohei, Koichi. *Book of Ki–Coordinating Mind and Body in Daily Life*, Japan Publications Inc, Tôkyô, 1976.

Tomita, Kaiji. *Reiki To Jinjutsu-Tomita Ryû Teate Ryôhô*, BAB Japan, Tôkyô, 1999.

Twan, Anneli. *Early Days of Reiki-Memories of Hawayo Takata*, Morning Star Productions, Hope, 2005.

Twan, Wanja. *In the Light of a Distant Star-A Spiritual Journey Bringing the Unseen into the Seen*, Morning Star Productions, Hope.

Turnbull, Stephen R. *Ninja-The True Story of Japan's Secret Warrior Cult*, Firebird Publishers, Belleville, 1992.

Unno, Taitetsu. *River of Fire–River of Water–An Introduction to the Pure Land Tradition of Shin Buddhism*, Doubleday, New

York, 1998.

Varley, Paul. *Japanese Culture*, University of Hawaii Press, Honolulu, 2000.

Watson, Burton. *The Lotus Sutra*, Columbia University Press, New York, 1993.

O

is a symbol of the world,
of oneness and unity. O Books
explores the many paths of wholeness
and spiritual understanding which
different traditions have developed down
the ages. It aims to bring this knowledge
in accessible form, to a general readership,
providing practical spirituality to today's seekers.

For the full list of over 200 titles covering:

- CHILDREN'S PRAYER, NOVELTY AND GIFT BOOKS
- CHILDREN'S CHRISTIAN AND SPIRITUALITY
- CHRISTMAS AND EASTER
- RELIGION/PHILOSOPHY
- SCHOOL TITLES
- ANGELS/CHANNELLING
- HEALING/MEDITATION
- SELF-HELP/RELATIONSHIPS
- ASTROLOGY/NUMEROLOGY
- SPIRITUAL ENQUIRY
- CHRISTIANITY, EVANGELICAL
  AND LIBERAL/RADICAL
- CURRENT AFFAIRS
- HISTORY/BIOGRAPHY
- INSPIRATIONAL/DEVOTIONAL
- WORLD RELIGIONS/INTERFAITH
- BIOGRAPHY AND FICTION
- BIBLE AND REFERENCE
- SCIENCE/PSYCHOLOGY

Please visit our website,
www.O-books.net

The Japanese Art of Reiki

Bronwen and *Frans Steine*

Reiki techniques originated in Japan, in an intensely spiritual period of that country's history. This fully-illustrated book traces the system's evolution from a spiritual self-development system to a direct hands-on practice. The journey moves from Japan to the USA, out to the world, and back to Japan.

Focussing on the basic elements in their historical context, this guide contains beautifully grounded information that captures a unique sense of the system's traditional Japanese roots. The clarity and accessibility of the teachings in the book redefine and strengthen the concept of Reiki as it is practised today.

Reiki Masters *Bronwen* and *Frans Steine* are the founders of the International House of Reiki. They have worked with Reiki and researched it for many years, their particular passion being the recovery of traditional Japanese Reiki. They live in Sydney, Australia.

1 90547 02 9

£12.99/$19.95

The Reiki Sourcebook

A comprehensive Reiki sourcebook

Bronwen and Frans Stiene

A balanced, respectful and up-to-date overview of Reiki history and practice, both in Japan and the West. Blissfully devoid of the extraneous fluff which fills so many other Reiki tomes. A MUST for any good practitioner and teacher.
James Wells, Reiki Master

One of the few Reiki books I can recommend: a complete guide to Reiki in its many guises, with the latest information about original Reiki from various sources, presented in a neutral and open way. Excellent.
Reiki Evolution eZine

Will satisfy anyone from novice to master. For me, it's most important contribution is to get as close as we possibly can, with the information we currently have, to Usui the man and Usui the seeker and teacher. I highly recommend it.
Pamir Kiciman, Oasis Reiki Institute

The definitive manual for teacher, student and general reader alike. Book News

The most complete work ever done on Reiki. The depth of the research is inspiring. Deserves its name.
A to Zen magazine

A comprehensive and professional guide, a must read for all Reiki followers. The Art of Healing

A wonderful book. William Lee Rand, author of *Reiki the Healing Touch*

An incredible job of researching and pulling the pieces together into a well-organised book. Kathleen Milner, author of *Reiki and Other ways of Touch Healing*

1 903816 55 6
£12.99/$19.95

Reiki Techniques Card Deck
Heal Yourself Intuitively
Bronwen & Frans Steine
Paperback with Card Deck in boxed set

You do not need to be a Reiki practitioner to benefit from this unusual healing card deck. Everyone on this planet has the ability to initiate self-healing-it is your birthright. The techniques in this deck of 45 cards, selected from the most effective traditional and non-traditional Reiki techniques from around the globe, offer you the opportunity to consciously tap into your healing ability, supporting you on your natural path.

What an incredible work. A must for all Reiki people. Mari Hall, founder and director of the International Association of Reiki

A gift to humanity. It de-clutters and demystifies so many misconceptions about Reiki. A "must" for fellow health-care practitioners.. Neil Anthony, UK Reiki Federation Chair and co-founder

You will fine EVERYTHING you would like to know about Reiki in this book, for this is the most updated and extensive work. This book will be highly appreciated and treasured. Inamoto Hyakuten, Japanese Reiki Master and founder of Komyo Reiki

Reiki Masters *Bronwen* and *Frans Stiene* are the founders
of the International House of Reiki and authors of
internationally acclaimed *The Reiki Sourcebook*.

1 90547 19 3
£15.99/$24.95